ROMAN WARSHIPS

ROMAN WARSHIPS

MICHAEL PITASSI

THE BOYDELL PRESS

First published in hardback 2011
Published in paperback 2019
The Boydell Press, Woodbridge
Transferred to digital printing 2020

ISBN 978 1 78327 414 7

The Boydell Press is an imprint of Boydell & Brewer Ltd
PO Box 9, Woodbridge, Suffolk IP12 3DF, UK
and of Boydell & Brewer Inc.
668 Mount Hope Ave, Rochester, NY 14620, USA
website: www.boydellandbrewer.com

A CIP catalogue record for this book is available
from the British Library

The publisher has no responsibility for the continued existence or accuracy of URLs for
external or third-party internet websites referred to in this book, and does not guarantee
that any content on such websites is, or will remain, accurate or appropriate.

Papers used by Boydell & Brewer Ltd are natural, recyclable products
made from wood grown in sustainable forests

Printed in Great Britain by
TJ International Ltd, Padstow, Cornwall

CONTENTS

ILLUSTRATIONS

The author and publishers are grateful to all the institutions and individuals listed for permission to reproduce the materials in which they hold copyright. Every effort has been made to trace the copyright holders; apologies are offered for any omission, and the publishers will be pleased to add any necessary acknowledgement in subsequent editions.

INTRODUCTION

O ften perceived as the poor relation of the army, the Roman Navy, in all of its various guises, whether Republican or Imperial, over the many centuries of its existence and in its disparate fleets, was in fact an extremely impressive and important force in its own right. At its height, it ruled the seas and the major river systems in and around Europe, Western Asia and North Africa; its squadrons ranged from the Black Sea to the Atlantic Ocean, from the north of Scotland to the western Sahara coastline. Not only that, but it exercised a power over those waters which was, for centuries, absolute; there simply were no other navies tolerated, a situation unknown by any other navy before, or indeed since.

It had not always been so, and the fleets had their ancestry in a few comparatively small and humble ships in the early fourth century BC, before growing to dominance by the mid-third century BC. This dominance was to last until the mid-third century AD, when a decline in strength, allied to increasing barbarian maritime activity from beyond the bounds of the Empire, started the process that would lead to its final extinction by the mid-fifth century AD. For approximately eight hundred years, therefore, hundreds and hundreds of Roman warships plied seas and rivers, evolving and changing all the while to meet different circumstances and the demands of a wide and changing variety of opponents and operating areas.

A warship is a complicated thing, and the building of a modern warship today, with all of its complexity, represents one of the highest expressions of technological ability. The same was also true two and a half millennia ago, pro rata to the technology of the day. Over the course of their long history, the Roman navies built, borrowed, adapted, invented and evolved a variety of warships for different tasks at different times and over a range of, and to suit, very different operational environments.

More than a thousand wrecks of ships from the period between the founding of Rome (753 BC) and the end of the Western Empire (AD 476) have so far been identified in the Mediterranean alone. However, with the exception of one or two fragments, no example of a seagoing Roman warship *per se* has yet been found. Furthermore, there survives no really accurate description or illustration of a Roman warship, sufficient for us to be able to unequivocally say 'that is what it actually looked like'. A few examples of river patrol craft have been found and excavated which are sufficiently complete to enable them to be imagined and realised in reconstructions with some considerable accuracy. For seagoing ships, however, questions remain, such as 'what did they actually look like?'; 'how did they work?'; 'what were they for and why were they as they were?'. One is then left with the difficulties of interpreting the few existing literary descriptions ('mentions' would be more accurate, since they lack detail), paintings and statuary of ships which is all that have come down to us to date.

This book is intended as an attempt to follow the evolution and development of Roman warships and to envisage examples of at least some of them, as they developed across the centuries. It comes largely from trying to produce examples of ships that conform to what is known about circumstances at the time and the operational requirements that led to their emergence. These examples must also conform to the appropriate iconography and literature, while still working when converted into three dimensions by way of a scale model. There have been several interpretations that work and look fine on paper, but which have had to be rethought and altered when 'in the round', as a result of some unforeseen problem. Contemporary evidence has been sought to substantiate each interpretation and the addition of details of fixture and fittings, some of it admittedly far less substantial than would have been ideal. All interpretations, in the absence of an example of a real ship being discovered, must of necessity and by definition be subjective, and one must always be careful not to jump to often tempting conclusions, nor to try to fit something around a preconceived idea. That said, it is hoped that these pitfalls have been avoided in what follows.

The term 'bulwark' has been preferred in describing a section of ship's side, rather than the currently common term 'gunwale', which seems singularly inappropriate for an age preceding the gun. The author is not and makes no pretension to be a naval architect, and the drawings are offered only as an attempt to give an overall impression of how these ships may have looked; they go no further than the available evidence will allow. Those more expert in the technicalities of boat and ship design will doubtless find fault with aspects and details of some of the interpretations proposed, but if these drawings can at least provide a reasonable starting point for such reconstructions, they will have proved sufficient. All interpretations offered are thus strictly those of the author and are put forward in the hope that they can be considered to show reasonably workable representations of their prototypes. No claim is made, nor can be made, that they are in any way definitive or the last word on the subject, which will always have to await the discovery, for each type, of an actual example of a Roman warship of sufficient completeness to settle the question once and for all.

Si vis pacis, para bellum

If you want peace, prepare for war
Vegetius

PART 1

INTERPRETATION

1

SOURCES

LITERATURE

At the risk of stating the obvious, any examination of a subject should preferably start with examples of the subject in question. In the case of ships and especially of wooden ships of such antiquity where, with the exceptions later mentioned, there are none extant, it is to the contemporary sources, written and physical, that one must turn to discover particulars of such vessels. Commencing with the surviving ancient literature, if soon becomes obvious that there is little in the way of detailed descriptions of warships. There are only a few exceptions, and one that comes to mind is Caesar, in his *Gallic Wars*,[1] describing the ships of the Celtic Venetii of Brittany but, frustratingly for us, failing to describe his own ships, presumably because the audience for whom he was writing were *au fait* with them. Warships are mentioned, for example, by Livy and Tacitus among others, but as part of their narrative only and are not described. Polybius, as a member of Scipio's entourage, actually voyaged on warships during the Third Punic War (149–146 BC) and Tacitus, in the late first century AD as part of Agricola's entourage, also saw and probably travelled on them. Both give few clues which would enable a picture of those warships to be formed.

However, it would be wrong to think that ancient authors can offer no insight into Roman warships, they are worthy of study for the odd snippet of information. Even the briefest mention can allow a detail to be gleaned. As an example, Livy describes a battle between some Roman and Carthaginian ships in 206 BC, in the Straits of Gibraltar,[2] when a Roman quinquereme overcame some Punic triremes, which, although faster, had less oarpower and could not manoeuvre so well in the strong current. In another example it was reported that marines could not board a quinquereme from a quadrireme as the former's deck was that much higher.[3]

There have been many modern attempts to establish just what an ancient warship looked like, both in books and by film-makers (it is worth noting, by the way, that Roman warships were not rowed by slaves such as in Ben Hur and rowers were certainly never chained to their benches: the 'galley slave' was an aberration of the sixteenth century AD and after). However fanciful some of the renditions may appear, they all will be found to have elements which can be attested to a greater or lesser degree and which look 'right'. They will also meet our two cardinal criteria, namely to accord with the sources and to have the ability to work in reality.

There have been some wonderful reproductions of ancient Greek ships built[4] or even converted from modern boats for books and such films as *Jason and the Argonauts* and more authentically, of course, the building of the reproduction Athenian trireme *Olympias*. The only time that a seagoing Roman warship has been attempted that comes to mind was when the French Emperor Napoleon III (r. 1852–70) commissioned his naval architect Depuy de Lome to build a quinquereme. The resulting ship was so heavy that it was nigh on impossible to row and after a few years it was expended as a gunnery target.

One can really only hope that one day an example of a Roman warship will be found, sufficiently well preserved to enable a definitive reconstruction. How fascinating to then be able to compare all the mass of speculation which has accumulated over the years, including that in this book, with actuality.

ICONOGRAPHY

There are several surviving types of illustration of Roman warships: statuary, mosaics, coins and wall paintings. All of them suffer, however, to varying degrees, from a discernable lack of accuracy, being impressionistic or stylised to accord with the qualities of the medium worked in, the exigencies of the arena of display or the artistic conventions of the time. Even time could play a role, for example in a wall painting executed on damp plaster (a fresco), speed was necessarily of the essence and compelled the artist to convey an impression only. Had it not been so done, however, those works would by now have long since ceased to exist and we would not have even those few impressions. Of one thing we can be sure, that there are, to date, no known surviving accurate, detailed drawings, diagrams or descriptions. In illustration of this, see Figures 1 and 2, two wall paintings of warships, the former still reasonably clear, while Figure 2 has been damaged or has simply deteriorated to an extent where it is only vaguely recognisable as a ship. We are left, therefore, with the need to interpret the renditions that do survive and to try to formulate interpretations of our own that, while embodying the elements shown, are reasonable and, above all, that would work in practice.

As for statuary, whereas proud owners of merchant ships seem to have commissioned altars, stelae and tomb-pieces showing their ships,[5] the Navy was more reticent, or at least so it appears from the very few pieces that survive. It is not always necessary to rely on the Navy *per se*. For instance a favourite theme of Etruscan funerary urns, for some obscure reason, was the tale of Odysseus and the Sirens, and there are many to be seen in Italian museums (Fig. 3). They are, in the small space used, extremely stylised and demonstrate an artistic convention common in the ancient world (and indeed later) of showing people on board ship exaggerated in size in relation to it. This is an important, constantly recurring convention that will affect interpretations and must be taken into account in rationalising the surviving depictions. These examples can nevertheless

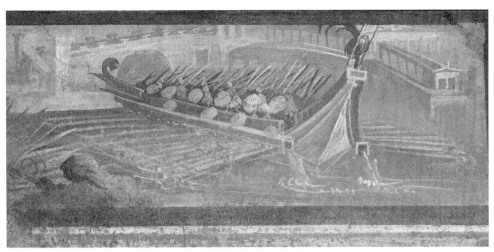

Figure 1. Detail from a wall painting from the Temple of Isis at Pompeii, mid-first century AD, which has been restored and remains in very good condition.

Figure 2. Wall painting in the House of the Golden Cupids, Pompeii, still in situ, which has badly deteriorated. A ship can still just be made out at upper left.

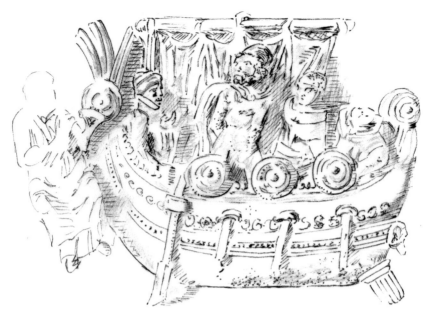

Figure 3. Detail from an Etruscan funerary urn., second century BC, showing a monoreme warship, very truncated to fit the stone, only a nominal three oars being represented and with the ram at an impossible angle.

Figure 4. A somewhat fanciful picture of a monoreme under full rig which could be a warship, a merchant galley or even a 'super yacht'. Part of a second- or third-century AD. mosaic from Tunisia.

Figure 5. Merchant galley. After a relief from a house in Rome.

Figure 6. Warships on coins. Above left: bronze denarius, Second Punic War period; above right: bronze denarius, 85 BC; below left: denarius of M. Agrippa, late first century BC; below right: denarius of M. Antonius as Triumvir, 43 to 36 BC.

provide details. For example, a bracket, presumably of metal, is shown for mounting the side rudder; one can also observe little details such as the shape of the steering oar and the rigels over the oar-ports and that no outrigger is portrayed.

Probably the most accurate and numerous surviving depictions of warships are those on the triumphal columns of the Emperors Trajan (AD 98–117) and Marcus Aurelius (AD 169–80) in Rome, although even here the exaggeration in size of the men on deck and the foreshortening of the ship hulls, necessitated by the available area and the curvature of the columns, has given rise to anomalies in the depiction of the ships (see Chapter 7). Nevertheless, once again, a study of these reliefs can provide significant amounts of information on the actual appearance of the ships, even if only over a limited period and in a limited theatre of operations.

There are many mosaics showing ships, most again being of merchant ships. A few (mostly in Tunisia) show what could be warships, although some of these are stylised in a way that could suggest they are pictures of the 'super yachts' of their day (Fig. 4). On this subject, a distinction must also be made between warships and merchant ships which were oar-powered (Fig. 5). Rowing merchant ships were used for perishable cargoes, for bringing exotic animals for the arenas and indeed, for any cargo that had to be moved fast.

Coins, among them some of the first ever issued by the Roman state, show warship prows and rams. Warship prows continued to be a popular subject for coin designs during the Republic and later. During the Civil War period and even in the Late Empire, whole ships were shown on coins (Figs. 6, 55, 81, 82 and 84). The problem with coins is, of course, their small size, which makes it impossible to convey anything but an overall impression of a ship. Once again, however, the odd detail may be discerned or the repetition of a particular item or shape could indicate a feature of the real thing or even a trend in warship design at a certain period and as such they are worth studying. A final advantage is that they are absolutely dateable.

There survive a few wall paintings of warships, most notably those from Pompeii and Herculaneum. As mentioned above, due to the medium in which they were painted they are impressionistic in style and, as will be discussed later, appear to fall into distinct types. They are nevertheless immensely valuable as dateable, contemporary depictions of the real thing and must be regarded as authentic impressions. The real thing could so easily be seen every day by the artists, going to and from the naval base at Misenum just across the bay. Another problem is that sometimes an ancient representation of a ship or even of a detail of it will appear to us to be totally wrong, even ridiculous, but whereas it is all too tempting to dismiss it as a flight of fancy, it may just be that it was right and one must avoid doing so without very careful consideration indeed (Fig. 7).

One of the biggest problems with the overall iconography is the lack of any continuity. There are huge time spans between illustrations, so, for example, for the first century AD, there are the Pompeii paintings, for the second century AD, the triumphal columns, but what did a third- or fourth-century AD Mediterranean warship look like? Similarly there are next to no illustrations of warships from the great Punic Wars period (third century

Figure 7. Did the ancient artist know what he was doing? The top illustration, from a vase, is generally accepted as depicting a fight between a Greek ship, on the left, and an Etruscan one, on the right. Although primitive in its execution, much useful detail is shown, for example the Greek helmsman is protected by a shield; the Etruscan ship has a crow's nest. The stars and 'flower' motifs could signify the fight in the same way that modern cartoonists still draw stars and 'explosions' in a fight or battle scene. However, surely a huge mistake has been made in the drawing of the bow and ram of the Etruscan ship, which seems all wrong and as opposed to that of the (more conventional) Greek ship. However, consider the prow of the Thai Royal Barge below it; perhaps that ancient artist got it right after all.

BC), when vast war-fleets plied the seas. For even earlier periods, reliance must be placed on painted Greek and Greek-style pottery. Once again, however, although these do not appear to specifically relate to Roman warships, they are extremely useful in showing the general appearance of contemporary ships. There is no reason to suppose that the comparatively few warships operated by the Romans in those times would have differed substantially. Pottery containers and vessels, including those showing ships, survive in considerable numbers, and there are collections in museums throughout southern Italy, where much of the pottery was made, as well as in Greece and elsewhere, for example at the British Museum. Other representations of warships may also appear in more unlikely forms, for example the lamp in Figure 44 and the model in Figure 49, and they were used for decoration of exotic drinking cups (rhytons) or as plinths for statues.[6]

ARCHAEOLOGY

It is to archaeology that one must turn to produce surviving examples or parts of them. Whereas the remains of many sunken Roman merchant ships have been located and excavated by underwater archaeology, apart from a few river craft which have been recovered from riverine mud, no example of what is incontestably a Roman seagoing warship has yet been found. Whereas a merchant ship, if holed or swamped, sank by being dragged down by the weight of its cargo and river craft, left stuck on a river bank, were buried by drifting mud, an ancient warship, of which hundreds were lost, simply did not sink. Warships were made of wood, which of course floats, apart from which the heaviest thing on board was the crew, who could be depended upon to get out and off if the ship was stricken.[7] Thus there was nothing in it heavy enough to overcome the latent buoyancy of the timber. When holed in battle by rams or wrecked they just settled to the waterline dictated by that latent buoyancy, useless for further combat and disabled; it was a 'perk' of the victor in a naval battle to tow away the wrecks.[8] If the unfortunate ship were wrecked in a storm or driven on to a coast, it would break up into bits and become just so much driftwood. Old, rotten, badly damaged or sometimes just surplus ships were burnt[9] or broken up for timber and firewood.

The wrecks and remains of many Roman seagoing ships have been found, ranging in period from the third century BC to the fifth century AD. They have been found in all kinds of environment, from beneath dry land that was once a harbour, as at Pisa[10] and Fiumicino,[11] to the deep seas, such as those found at over 2,400 feet (750m) down, north-west of Sicily.[12] Between such extremes and off coasts, such examples as the Mahdia wreck from Tunisia and the Grand Ribaud wreck from the French coast and others have come to light. From England to Turkey,[13] ships and boats of all types have been and continue to be found which have one thing in common, namely a mercantile provenance.[14] Despite the hopes that some of the remains gave rise to, no unequivocal identification of any seagoing warship has been possible. Any reconstruction of the appearance of, for instance, a quinquereme can still rely only on surviving iconography and literary references, with all of their respective shortcomings, which will be examined later.

In relation to river craft, the position is much better, several examples having been excavated from the Rhine and upper Danube area of sufficiently complete vessels from different periods, to allow a positive identification as warships.[15] These ships and boats have been preserved by having been (fortuitously) abandoned or dumped on a river bank, where the rising accretion of mud and silt has served to preserve them. Thus they did not 'sink' but the river bank built itself up around and over them. Enough has been recovered to provide the basis for full-size reproductions.

One of the most important results of the continuing archaeology and the examination of the finds of the remains of ancient ships, has been to demonstrate how the shipwrights of the ancient world practised their trade. From early times, throughout the ancient Mediterranean, ship hulls were built 'shell-first'. The shipwrights having fashioned and set out the keel, stem and stern posts next fitted the garboard strakes, the first plank of the hull skin on either side of the keel. They then proceeded to fashion and fit each succeeding plank or strake on either side to build up the outer hull, holding it with jigs and spacers as they went, these being for guidance only and were all removed when the shell of the hull was complete. At that stage, frames, thwarts and strengthening timbers were permanently fitted inside the hull. The hull planks or strakes were joined edge to edge by cutting a great number of closely spaced mortices or slots at matching intervals in the mating edges of the planks to be joined, then fitting a wooden tenon into each mortice on one plank, next fitting the other plank to it, thereby engaging its mortices over the tenons in the preceding strake. With the two planks pushed together to a tight fit, holes were drilled through each plank and tenon and a wooden dowel driven through to secure each joint (Fig. 8).[16]

This method yielded a strong hull, relatively free from built-in stress and needing little or no caulking (for which tow was used[17]). On the other hand it was extremely labour-intensive – imagine having to bevel the edge of a long, thin plank to match a compound curve along the edge of its mating piece, not to mention chopping literally hundreds of accurate mortices, all by hand in the thin edge, only a few inches in thickness. It required highly skilled shipwrights and was wasteful of materials, as much as three-quarters of a piece of timber could be cut away to fashion it into a fit. The use of this construction method has nevertheless been traced back to at least 1350 BC, the date of the oldest wreck so far found to be built in this way.[18] It would continue in use with little change for both merchant ships and warships until at least the end of the third century AD.[19] The method, or variations of it, has continued in use in various parts of the world, down to the present day.

Hulls were smeared inside and out with pitch or a mixture of pitch and tar (from natural tar ponds) or wax and lime to protect them from marine parasites.[20] Later, merchant ship hulls were further protected by thin lead sheathing, laid over tarred fabric and fixed by nails, a method that added too much weight for use by a warship and which would hamper its speed.[21] Wax-based paints were made with pigments to provide white, purple, blue, yellow, red, brown and green.[22] With the primary colours, any other colour could also be mixed.

For building the ships, pine, fir, oak, elm and more exotic woods such as cedar

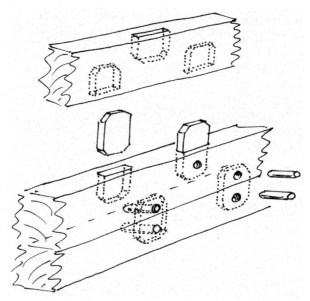

Figure 8. Sketch of a section of hull showing mortice and tenon method of hull construction.

and cypress were used as well as beech, larch and, in fact, whatever else was available locally.[23] Frequent mention is made[24] of ships being built using freshly cut 'green' or unseasoned timber. One would tend to think this a reckless practice, as the timber, as it becomes seasoned, could be expected to twist, crack, shrink and generally move about dramatically, ruining a hull, especially as, for the most part, highly 'mobile' fir, pine and cypress was used, added to hardwoods such as oak for keels, stem and stern posts and tenons, with each moving at a differing rate and in a different direction. However, more recent experience[25] has demonstrated that green timber was preferred, being much easier to work and fashion and being the more supple.[26] It was for the shipwrights to gauge the probable future conduct of a piece of timber as it aged and to use it in a manner that would allow for this. A further factor for the shipwright to consider was that green timber has a higher moisture content than seasoned wood, but that it will become lighter as it seasons. Further allowance thus had to be made so that the ship would float to its correct waterline once the hull timbers had become seasoned. This was particularly critical for a warship, as the height of the oar-ports and tholes above the water directly affected whether it could be rowed efficiently, or even, in extreme cases, at all. Further, in a warship, the luxury of adjustment of the waterline by the addition of ballast, which would slow it, was to be avoided.[27] That this was done successfully for so many centuries for hundreds, if not thousands, of ships of all types says a great deal about the degree of accumulated experience and skill acquired and required of the shipwrights of the ancient world.

Rope was made from flax, papyrus reed or hemp, as well as from esparto grass.[28] Sails were made from canvas woven from flax or hemp,[29] both of which are indigenous to western Asia and Europe and in various weights, from heavy-duty to lightweight. Cotton, indigenous to India and central Asia, also spread and was increasingly grown in Egypt (it still is) and used for light-weather sails and awnings.[30]

To quickly provide the numbers that were used, mass-production methods for building warships were evolved, and archaeological evidence has indicated that parts of ships were prefabricated to standardised designs.[31] The use of jigs upon which they could be set up and formed seems a logical deduction. In this way, parts could be and were made *en masse* by non-specialist manufacturers and transported to the shipyards for assembly, as was done during the World Wars. Timber baulks could be cut to specified sizes and preformed at the lumber yards, and, given a pattern, a sail or an oar, for example, could be made anywhere.[32] At times of peak construction, as for example in the First Punic War, shipyards resembled assembly plants to a greater extent than usual.

By the mid-first century AD shipbuilding methods started to change, in that the previously closely spaced mortice and tenon joints became more widely spaced and thus a little cheaper and quicker in construction.[33] Perhaps it had been found that such close spacing of the joints, unless made with the very best-quality timber, could actually weaken it; perhaps that such close spacing simply was not necessary; it may even have been cost that dictated that change take place. The spacing seems to have become progressively wider and increasingly used primarily to locate and position the hull planking, with a correspondingly increasing reliance for the actual strength and integrity of the hull placed upon the increased use of built-up frames or ribs. By about the late third century AD, around the Mediterranean, ships were being built totally 'frame-first', that is by first building a 'skeleton', which was then clad, the former now giving the hull form and strength and being the method in general use ever since.[34] This method of building a ship hull was the total opposite of the original method. In northern Europe, the 'plank-on-frame' method had evolved and was in use much earlier. It may even have been employed in the Gallic ships that were opposed by and described by Caesar.[35] The method was certainly in use in the mid-second century AD, as evidenced by the 'Blackfriars ship' of that time, discovered in the River Thames in London, which was built in this way. The 'County Hall ship' of the late third century AD, also found in the Thames in London, which had been built somewhere on the English Channel was however, built using the mortice and tenon system; obviously the two methods coexisted at least until then.

Fastenings were of hardwood dowel, copper (which reacts badly to the corrosive effect of seawater and had to be renewed), bronze (expensive and used more for fittings that showed) and iron, the latter being more widely used later in the period.[36] To avoid the risk of splitting hull timbers by the driving in of nails, a hole was first bored, then filled by a softwood plug (a treenail) and the nail was driven into the plug, which was compressed to form a firm fixing. Some hulls (of merchant ships, of course) have been found to have been patched by way of repair to damage or to replace some soft timber, and some also have been either built with or have subsequently had added a second, complete skin of hull planking, secured over the first, the result being a very strong, if heavy, hull.[37]

Some of the ships had, by our standards, very long service lives; the wreck of one Roman merchantman discovered off Taranto was over a hundred years old when lost,[38] and the wreck of a small merchantman found off Kyrenia in Cyprus was some eighty years old when lost. The huge flagship of Philip of Macedon's fleet, a 'sixteen' which had been built in about 296 BC, was taken by the Romans in 167 BC and although by then over 120 years old, they sailed her from the northern Aegean to Rome to display as a trophy and to take part in the victory celebrations. It has been argued that this was not all the same ship, but a 'sixteen' was an extremely rare beast and it is fair to assume that they were one and the same.[39]

The shipbuilding methods outlined above have been gleaned from examination of non-warship types and can thus only be assumed to have been employed in the building of warships. However, it is a reasonably safe assumption, in that it would be strange if two different construction regimes were applied, depending upon whether a warship or a merchant ship was being built. As confirmation of this, firstly, a bronze ram was recovered from the sea off Athlit in Israel with parts of the hull to which it had been fitted still attached and which had been built in this fashion;[40] secondly, parts of the hulls of what are believed to be two Carthaginian warships have been recovered from western Sicily which date from the First Punic War period (264–241 BC), both built on the mortice and tenon, 'shell-first' principle.[41] Ironically, and confirming the contention above as to the 'unsinkability' of ancient warships, these were both found to be loaded with (and sunk by) cargoes of stone, identified as originating from mainland Italy. The inference is that they were Punic ships, captured by the Romans and intended to be sunk by them as blockships to close the nearby harbour of Lilybaeum (Marsala), which they were then besieging.[42]

NOTES

1 Caesar, *The Battle for Gaul* III.13.
2 Livy, VIII.30.
3 Polybius, XV.2.
4 Such as the 'Kyrenia' ship; the *Argo*; from a later period, the 'Yassi Ada' ship.
5 Examples can be found, for example at Pompeii, Bacoli and Split.
6 There is a splendid example of the former in the British Museum and examples of the latter in the Louvre, in Libya and in Sicily.
7 That crews of a stricken ship were expected to escape is perhaps proved by the exceptions where they could not, unusual enough to justify mention in the ancient sources, for example Caesar, *Civil War* II.1, 6, 7.
8 For example, Livy, XXII.20.

9 For example, the fate of the surrendered Carthaginian fleet, Livy, XXX.43 and the disposal of surplus ships after Actium in 31 BC.

10 The site of the ancient harbour of Pisa with the remains of more than sixteen ships and boats ranging in date from the fifth century BC to the fourth century AD was discovered in 1998 little more than 800 yards (732 m) from the Leaning Tower.

11 Where five ships and boats were recovered from the area of Claudius' and Trajan's harbours at Porto.

12 The Skerki Bank Deep Water Project which, using remotely operated exploration vehicles, found and mapped five ancient merchant ship wrecks.

13 For example the 'Blackfriars ship' found in a bank of the Thames in London, and see Bass, *A History of Seafaring*.

14 For a listing, see Navis, a database of ancient ships found; also the Oxford Roman Economy Project shipwreck database, both on the Internet.

15 The remains of five such craft are preserved near to where they were discovered, at the Museum of Ancient Shipping, Mainz, the former Roman base of Moguntiacum. Two more were found near the headwaters of the Danube and are also preserved at Mainz. See Chapters 6 and 8.

16 See Bass, *A History of Seafaring* and Casson, *Ships and Seamanship*.

17 Traces of which have been found, see above.

18 The 'Cape Gelidonya' wreck, see Bass, *A History of Seafaring*; much earlier and less developed versions can be seen in the Egyptian 'Dashur' boats of *c.* 1850 BC, and see Ward, *Sacred and Secular*.

19 For more modern examples of this method of construction, see Severin, *The Jason Voyage*, on the building of the *Argo*, and Morrison, Coates and Rankov, *The Athenian Trireme* on the building of the *Olympias*. The 'County Hall ship' discovered in the River Thames in London and dated to the late third century AD is also built in this way.

20 See Casson, *Ships and Seamanship*, quoting Procopius.

21 Caligula's barges, recovered from Lake Nemi, were so sheathed, over a layer of pitch and bitumen, which is curious as they were fresh-water craft, remote from the sea's parasites. Scale models of these ships, showing the sheathing, with some fragments of it, can be seen in the Naval Museum, La Spezia.

22 Vegetius, IV.37; surviving wall paintings show them painted. See also Herodotus, III.58.

23 From analysis of wrecks recovered, see Bass, *A History of Seafaring*; Welsh, *Building the Trireme*, quoting Theophrastus: Livy, XXVIII.45; Vegetius, IV.34 and so on. Herodotus, II.96, mentions the use of acacia wood by the Egyptians.

24 For example, Livy, XXVIII.46; Theophrastus as before.

25 Severin, *The Jason Voyage*; also Welsh, *Building the Trireme*; Morrison, Coates and Rankov, *The Athenian Trireme*, for accounts of recently built reproductions, using the ancient system.

26 Theophrastus (quoted in Casson, *Ships and Seamanship*) states 'in shipbuilding, because bending is necessary, wood which is rather green must be used'.

27 Livy, XXIX.1: new ships had to be hauled ashore as they could not be left afloat in winter, unlike the older ships. Contrast Vegetius, IV.36, who maintains the opposite, i.e. that only seasoned wood should be used; however, by his time, methods had changed and ships were being built 'frame-first' (see below).

28 Casson, *Ships and Seamanship*, quoting ancient writers; Livy, XXVI.47 specifically mentions esparto grass from Spain.

29 Caesar, *The Battle for Gaul* III.13; Livy, XXVIII.45.

30 Herodotus, III.47, mentions 'tree-wool' in use by the people of Samos in the mid-sixth century BC, so perhaps it was being grown in other areas of the eastern Mediterranean by then.

31 The remains of two ships found off Marsala (see below) have shipwright's assembly marks cut into the timbers; Livy, XXVIII.45 again, mentions 'timber for keels'.

32 Livy once more, at XXVIII.45.

33 See Bass, *A History of Seafaring* and Casson, *Ships and Seamanship*.

34 The *lusoria*, detailed later, was built frame-first.

35 Caesar, *The Battle for Gaul* III.13

36 Vegetius, IV.34. Nails and fixings have been recovered from wrecks, see, e.g. Bass, *A History of Seafaring*. The exclusion of any air by mud or silt has prevented the process of corrosion.

37 See Casson, *Ships and Seamanship*.

38 The 'Torre Sgarrata' wreck; the timber for it was felled *c.* AD 50 and the ship contained coins dated AD 192, Bass, *A History of Seafaring*; Thubron, *The Seafarers*.

39 The saga of this ship can be traced through Polybius, e.g. XVIII.44.

40 For a full description, see Casson and Steffy, *The Athlit Ram*.

41 For a full description, see Frost, 'The Punic Wreck in Sicily'.

42 Polybius, I.47.

2

INTERPRETING THE SOURCES

THE LITERARY SOURCES

There are many references in ancient literature to ships and shipping and all manner of matters nautical, regrettably, however, many of them are unclear, inconsistent or ambiguous. It must also be borne in mind that after some two thousand years, original copies have long gone and what survives is the result of successive copies made over the centuries since (all copied by hand until the advent of the printing press in the fifteen century AD), with all the consequent possibilities for errors and mistranslations to have corrupted the original text. Further ancient terms and usages will have become changed, forgotten or simply disused, thereby adding to the problems of later copiers and translators. Problems can easily arise, therefore, when we wish to interpret what has come down to us of the ancient sources, as it is not always a simple thing to ascertain what they may have meant at the time. Some are quite easy, and apparent inconsistencies can be overcome by deduction. Thus, for example, the rank of *trierarch* (Greek), obviously the commander of a trireme, was a rank which was latterly applied as the term for the commander or captain (a word from Latin) of any warship, irrespective of the man's actual rank. It is exactly the same way that today a lieutenant put in command of a ship becomes the captain of that ship even though he does not hold that rank in the naval hierarchy. Other terms are not so clear: what was a 'ten'?[1] It was a ship, in fact, and a big one, but how did it work and what did the number signify? Similarly, the ancient trireme, it is generally accepted, was rowed by groups of three men, each at one of three horizontal levels (remes); confusion then arises when the term was resurrected and applied to a Renaissance galley, when three men rowed from the same bench, all at the same level – the same term but a different application.

The translation or transliteration of terms relating to ancient warships is an area littered with academic argument, but one which, without the addition of 'hard' evidence – that is to say the real thing or more definitive discoveries, at least – remains largely speculative.[2]

Many of the terms that survive emanate from the Greeks and were adopted and 'latinised' by the Romans, who added Etruscan and their own terms to the nautical vocabulary that has come down to us. The Greeks classified their warships in two main ways, firstly by reference to the number of oars by which they were propelled,[3] and then by a number, such as *triereis*[4] (literally 'three-fitted'), and so on in succession, up to forty.

In the first case, three terms seem to have been used for the type of ship rowed by a number of men, sitting one behind the other along each side of the ship. Such a ship was called an *eikosoros*,[5] *eikose* being the Greek word for twenty and thus, literally, a 'twenty-er'. As the ships grew beyond that in size and motive power, two more terms were applied in the sequence, namely the *triakontoros*[6] ('thirty-er') and *pentekontoros*[7] ('fifty-er'). *Kontoros* is usually rendered as 'conter' in English, these terms referring to ships of twenty, thirty and fifty oars respectively. This seems straightforward, except that the extant illustrations of ships that appear to be of this general type, mostly on pottery vessels, rarely show such convenient round numbers of oars, examples showing, for instance, thirty-two and forty-four oars (Fig. 9). The solution would seem to be to simply regard the terms as referring in fact to ships 'of up to twenty oars' and of 'between twenty and thirty oars' and of 'thirty to fifty oars'.

The problems multiply with the further development of warships and the change to the second system of classifying types. Starting with the *triereis*, which to the Romans became the trireme. *Reme* is the Latin word for an oar (*kope* in Greek, *un ramo* in modern Italian), not a row or file of *remiges* or oarsmen (which is an *ordine* in Latin). The Greeks therefore had three fittings of some sort, which the Romans translated literally as three oars. As another example the terms 'monoreme', 'bireme' and 'trireme' are generally and not unreasonably used by modern writers (and will be so used in this book), and the second two by ancient writers as well, to refer to ancient ships propelled by one, two and three horizontal levels or remes of oars respectively. However, if the terms are used literally, monoreme equals one oar, bireme equals two oars and trireme equals three only and around we go in another circle (the terms will nevertheless be used in this book in their generally accepted meanings). This is clearly nonsense, but serves to illustrate the type of pitfalls and the problem remaining, namely what did the terms mean over two thousand years ago? Three is the maximum number of levels/remes mentioned and illustrated in the ancient sources, and only three classifications of rower are known.

The numbering system was used for ships rated from three to forty, the largest type known to have been engaged in a battle being a 'sixteen'.[8] The Romans used up to 'sixes',[9] but what do these numbers signify? It is generally accepted that they refer to the number of fore-and-aft files of rowers on each side of a ship's beam; so the trireme has three files, a cross-section of the ship revealing three men each with an oar, on each side, six files in all. Thus a quinquereme had five men (with some oars manned by more than one man each) on each side, five fore-and-aft files, ten in total in the cross-section. There are, however, good reasons for questioning why those ancient mariners should refer to a 'three' or a 'four' and so forth, when they were in fact referring to a ship with double that number of files. There again, they also referred to a 'hemiolia', or one and a half, and a 'trihemiolia', or three and a half, whatever they may have been. One can only conclude that it was a convention of the time and that the 'group' (threes, fours, sevens, etc.) was regarded as a sub-unit of the rowing crew, perhaps with a leading hand in charge.

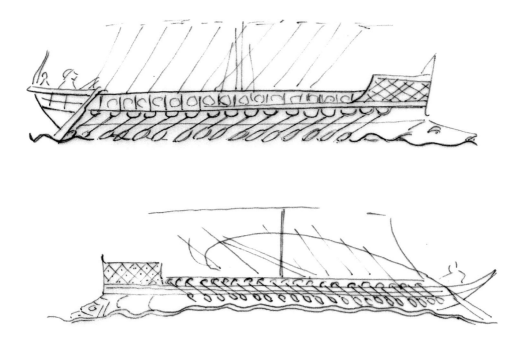

Figure 9. After Greek pottery vessels showing monoreme conters, the upper with sixteen oars, the lower with twenty-two oars per side. Sixth century BC.

Figure 10. Extract from graffito at Alba Fucens in Central Italy, with the only known 'type label' of a Roman warship to date. Probably first century BC or AD.

About the only thing beyond doubt is that the bigger the number, the bigger the ship, because that much at least we are told. However, just to complicate things even more, towards the end of the wars between the various successors to Alexander the Great, when the 'super' galleys had grown beyond a 'twenty', a new type, called an 'eight', was introduced and trounced the older polyremes. A similar situation arose in the Roman world in AD 324 when Constantine's 'triaconters' roundly defeated Licinius' fleet of triremes (see Chapter 8). The possibility of assigning a particular description to a particular representation of a ship must remain a matter of pure guesswork, albeit of a more or less educated nature, as, with one exception, none is labelled 'this is picture of a such-and-such' or the like. The exception is a graffito at Alba Fucens in central Italy of a '*navis tetreris longa*' which is incomplete and of indeterminate date but probably first century BC or AD and which is accordingly assumed to show a type known as a 'long four' and which is in itself an amalgam of Latin and Greek words (Fig. 10).

Another problem in using the 'old' terms is that they, or at least some of them, changed in meaning over the course of the several centuries that they were in use. Just as, for example, our modern warship type, the frigate, has changed from the light scouting ship used for long-range patrols and raiding in Nelson's time two centuries ago to the smallish, primarily anti-submarine escort ship of the World Wars and from that to the general-purpose medium-sized warship of today, so the liburnian of the Romans changed from (apparently) a smallish open rowing craft from the Dalmatian coast, to a light, scouting warship, to a full-bodied, two-level or bireme for seagoing use, until the term seems to have become applied fairly indiscriminately to virtually all warships,[10] in much the same way every modern warship is a 'battleship' to some modern journalists.

THE ICONOGRAPHY

It is not unreasonable to make the assumption that, for the most part, those artists and craftsmen of old more or less knew what they were doing in representing warships. Allowing for the media in which they worked, the limits imposed by their apparent incomplete understanding of perspective and, of course, the artistic and stylistic conventions of their times, they did indeed show what a warship looked like. After all, in such locations as the Bay of Naples, the artist had only to glance across the bay to see the real thing.

For this reason, it is proposed that prime reliance should be placed on the 'hard evidence' of contemporary pictorial representation. Should this coincide with or in any way accord with the written accounts or terms, so much the better, such corroboration and consensus strengthening the evidence for an interpretation.

In depicting a warship, or anything else for that matter, the craftsman of ancient times was faced with constraints upon the accurate and detailed portrayal that we should like to see now. In the case of sarcophagi or funerary monuments, the types or quality of stone used rarely permitted fine detail, which was, in any event, probably not required at the time;[11] in wall paintings, work had to be done quickly, usually on damp plaster (fresco) and was intended to give an impression rather than realistic portrayal; paintings on pots and other decorative pottery was complicated by the compound curvature of the vessel; mosaic could be almost photographic at its finest when used for portraits, but this quality never seems to have been applied to ships. As an example of what could be achieved, some of the ships shown on Trajan's Column in Rome are excellent in their detail and largely all that one could wish for. Even here, however, there are anomalies, which will be discussed later; it is also an example of the common artistic convention that required the ships to be shown with people aboard and of a size vastly exaggerated in comparison with the ship itself.

Another problem which manifests itself, particularly in wall paintings, is that an incomplete understanding of perspective leads to some very strange views and angles of ships and parts of ships (Fig. 11). Many wall paintings and even mosaics show ships with decks crammed to overflowing with soldiery, more than one would expect from their normal complement of marines and which, if converted to reality, would give the unfortunates no room to move at all. Too many men on deck would in addition add to top-weight and instability, especially if they all moved together. Tacitus records an instance with untrained men on a deck where the ship 'swayed with their movements and the rowers and fighters fell over each other in confusion'.[12] How much easier and quicker and visually quite effective it was, rather than having to detail small deck fittings and the like, to simply paint a mass of discs and straight lines to indicate soldiers bearing shields and spears (Fig. 12).

Once allowances are made for these problems and the above is not an exhaustive list, a comparison of several renditions of what appear to be similar types can lead to a consensus view with which the problems can be more or less resolved. A reasonable example of an actual ship can hopefully emerge which looks good and even as though it might work in real life.

THE PARAMETERS

In interpreting the available material, it must be borne in mind that the design of the ancient warship was dictated above all by the geometry of the human body and the way and the extent to which it could exert itself to pull and push an oar for an extended period. The designers and builders of old were always constrained by the rule that all dimensions must conform to those of the human body because the 'engines' of ancient warships were the rowers and it was around the accommodation of them that the ship was formed.

The next consideration must have been how to maximise the efficient use of rowers and their oars. The first problem is that an oar works most efficiently when it is close to the horizontal. The amount by which it must be lifted to clear the water at the end of a stroke is minimal, whereas the length of that stroke utilising the maximum blade area is at its greatest; unfortunately it is also essential for good sea-keeping to have as much freeboard (the distance between the water and the lowest level of the top of the

Figure 11. Part of a wall painting from the Temple of Isis at Pompeii, showing ships in an impossible situation, probably to the result of a poor understanding of perspective.

Figure 12. Detail from a Pompeii wall painting showing simple painted devices to indicate decks packed with marines.

ship's side or apertures such as oar-ports) as possible, a requirement which is in direct opposition to the desirability of a near-horizontal oar. It may be all very well in a flat calm for an oarsman to be close to the water, but as soon as waves appear the water will quickly start to come aboard.

Conversely, the more vertically an oar has to be operated, the more difficult and less efficient this becomes (there are of course exceptions, such as the gondola, which employs a totally different method of rowing) and the more difficult to raise the blade clear of the water at the end of each stroke. As evidence of this, the topmost or thranite oars of the trireme *Olympias* were at thirty degrees from the horizontal when in calm water and, as such, 'uncomfortable' in operation.[13] Therefore, for our purpose this could be adopted as a maximum permissible angle. Obviously these opposing requirements must be balanced by compromise and consideration of the environment and roles for which the ship is intended.

In the single-level 'conter' type of hull these matters can be reasonably easily overcome as the ship is comparatively small, and a freeboard of a couple of feet (600mm) or so can be comfortably combined with quite short oars, operated over the bulwark at a modest angle. It is, after all, only an extended rowing boat.

It is when a second level of oars is superimposed that the complications multiply. Being higher in the hull and further above the water, the triangle formed for the upper-level rowers between sea level, the pivot point of the oar and the point at which the blade pierces the water is totally different from that of the original (lower) level. If the men of the upper level sit inboard (that is, closer to the centre line) of those in the lower,[14] their oars, if of the same length, cannot reach the water, so why not just make them longer so that they can? The answer is that the upper and lower oar strokes cannot then be synchronised, and if this cannot be done, the oars will become fouled by each other and any thought of movement become lost in the ensuing shambles. There is an impeccable authority for the principle, namely one Barras de la Penne, the captain of the galleys of Louis XIV of France.[15] Small variations are acceptable, but the oars must all be of roughly the same length. To further emphasise the point, the surviving inventories for ancient Athenian triremes specify oar lengths for the ships as nine cubits and some at nine and one half cubits (the difference is about eight inches/210mm), the longer for use by the amidships rowers to compensate for the curve of the hull side and ensure that all blades struck the water uniformly.[16] To satisfy the geometry required to achieve this, therefore, the upper level must be sat to some degree outboard of the lower.

The other essential for synchronised oar working is in the gearing of the oar, that is the ratio or relationship between that part of the oar between its pivot point (the thole) and the end held by the rower (the loom) and the part from the thole to the end of the blade (the sweep). Given that the average seated rower, on a fixed seat, can pull his end of the oar through a certain arc, which is of course fixed by the size of a body at the stretch, to an average of, say, 4 feet 6 inches (1.37m), although for prolonged rowing, and in order not to tire the rowers quickly, 3 feet 6 inches (1.06m) is more realistic, the extent to which this is converted by the oar blade at the other end to useful propulsive power is dependent upon these respective lengths. Geometry again, but this time in the horizontal plane. Rowers in ancient times are known to have rowed whilst seated and although it lay within their technological ability, there is no evidence that sliding seats were used. In later times (fifteenth to eighteenth centuries AD) the rowers rose to their feet, then fell back, pulling their oar, to deliver the stroke (see Fig. 17). It is of course possible that some of the ancient systems required some or all of the men manning a large oar to do the same – there simply is no evidence available.

The longer the outboard sweep, as a multiple of the inboard loom, the larger an arc it will describe in the water on each stroke. Unfortunately, although the weight of the oar itself can be easily neutralised by a suitable weight mounted on the inboard end, the longer it becomes, the greater the effort required to overcome the inertia arising from the increased mass of oar and thus the harder it is to pull through the water. The mass of a huge oar will clearly reduce the frequency with which oar-strokes can be made, the 'striking rate'; over thirty per minute was achieved in the reconstruction of the Athenian trireme, whereas twenty-six has been suggested as the maximum for a Renaissance galley.[17] Once more, compromise must be sought in the gearing of the oar to give an oar that can be pulled with reasonable ease for an extended period, yet be capable of doing useful work. An oar divided one third of its length inboard and two thirds outboard works well (a gearing of 3.3, calculated by dividing the loom into the overall length of the oar)[18] and the gearing can go up to about four and a half before the oar becomes too tiring to pull and each stroke too long in length and time. Any shorter and the stroke becomes too short to do any useful work, being in the water for too short a time.

It can be readily seen how the problems multiply yet again if a third level of rowers is superimposed. There is no evidence that any more than three levels were used, presumably the limits of operability of an oar due to the increased acuteness of the angle needed to get it into the water and out again, rendering anything higher than this unuseable, quite apart from the question of added top-weight contributing in turn to instability. A final point on gearing is that each level of rowers sat above and outboard of the other, and must have their respective tholes positioned to maintain the same gearing for each, otherwise, once more, the oar-stroke cannot be synchronised. The necessity of a synchronised oar-stroke arises for several reasons, the first being that the maximum thrust of the oars is provided by them all passing through the water at the same time, rather than dissipating their effort by pulling at random. Secondly, the maximum number of oarsmen were accommodated in a very limited space, as an increase in motive power can only be obtained by increasing the number of oars per foot length of the hull; obviously being in such close proximity, the rowers had to move as one. Finally, simply imagine the chaos if the eighty-five oars along one side of a trireme, say, all tried to row at a different rate or indeed with anything less than perfect synchronisation.

It is not only in the vertical that limits were imposed on ancient warships, but also the horizontal, dictated by a measurement called the interscalmium (*skalmos*, Greek for thole): this is the distance, fore and aft, between a thole and the next one on the same level. Obviously all of the rowers moved back and forth together as they rowed, and although they could be placed closer together than the extent of their oar-stroke, nevertheless there needs to be enough room to allow for easy movement, different sizes of rowers and also space, let us not forget, for the circulation of air between them, an important point that will be returned to later. Less has been tried, [19] but has served only to reinforce the 'rule-of-thumb' that about 3 feet (920mm) is the minimum inter-scalmium, a figure borne out by such evidence as survives. Likewise, the width of the rower must be considered, and 2 feet (610mm) seems reasonable enough to allow for the broad-shouldered. Another parameter dictating the accommodation of rowers is that they worked while seated. The iconography (as on the Lenormant relief, Fig. 15) shows seated oarsmen, and there are plenty of literary references (corroboration and confirmation as mentioned earlier) to rowers reporting for duty carrying, obviously, their oar in one hand, but in the other clutching a seat cushion.[20] Each rower will thus, when seated, occupy a 'box' about 3 feet long by 2 feet wide and by up to 4 feet 6 inches high (920 × 610 × 1370mm) when stationary.

Having resolved the parameters of the 'engine room' in the middle, allowance must be made for a sharp bit at the front and a blunt bit at the back. Forward must be shaped to cleave the water, fine to give minimum resistance, yet sturdy enough to mount the ram and flared toward the deck above to allow room for the working of the ship and for some marines or archers in the bow. Aft the hull must again be fine to allow a clean path through the water, but with provision for mounting the steering gear. With all of this, however, the length of the ship must be related to its beam.

Returning to the 'conter' type of ship, adding extra rowers in a progressively length-ening ship was all very well but resulted in a long, skinny vessel that took a long time and a lot of space to turn – the manoeuvrability was very poor. Further, at more than twenty-five rowers per side, the ship became structurally deficient, being too slender for its beam. It was found that a length of ten times the beam was the maximum ratio that could be applied, and even that was more than was comfortable.[21] The long, thin hull is obviously faster through the water, or rather through calm water, but, and here we meet compromise again, the need for adequate sea-keeping requires an optimised length-to-beam ratio, and 8 to 1 was adopted at least for triremes by the ancients, as confirmed by the dimensions of the ship-sheds built to house them.[22] Even the Italian and French galleys of medieval and later times settled upon the same ratio.[23] Modern warships continue to use a similar ratio.[24]

Next to be considered is the depth of the hull in the water, the draft. Too little and the ship will bob about like a cork, too much and it will be too heavy in the water to move well or fast. Once again, and doubtless arising from a process of trial and error, a ratio emerged of between a quarter and not more than half of the beam.[25]

Finally, as to the height of the ship above the water, we are told that the deck of a quinquereme was 10 (Roman) feet above water level (about 9 feet 8 inches/2.95m)[26] and that this was higher than the deck of quadriremes and triremes.[27] Ships larger than fives presumably were higher but probably by little more than was needed to clear their rowing systems. There are reports of the height of these bigger ships being a factor in naval battles, both where it has been an advantage and, conversely, where they have fallen prey to smaller types.[28] Further, localised height would be gained by the installation of fighting towers and raised platforms on the decks, mindful always of the risks of added top-weight.

OAR SYSTEMS

There survives much iconography showing ships rowed by a line of oars all mounted at the same horizontal level and a number of rowers, as opposed to paddlers, each behind the other along the sides of a ship. It ranges in date from *c.* 3000 BC (Egyptian) through the Minoan and Mycenean eras, *c.* 2000 to 1000 BC and into the early ancient period (eighth century BC) and indeed beyond (Fig. 13). For convenience, they are referred to as monoreme in this book, although the term was unknown to the ancients.

The earliest depiction so far known of a ship rowed at two horizontal levels, the one superimposed above the other, is from Nineveh, the capital of ancient Assyria. Although the city was many miles from the sea, these images do have the inestimable benefit of inscriptions to exactly date and place the scene depicted, to the Phoenician coast *c.* 710 BC (Fig. 14).[29] Two-level ships are subsequently shown by the Greeks, Etruscans and Romans over the course of the centuries up to the end of the ancient world, all of which will be referred to as biremes.

As for ships rowed at three horizontal, superimposed levels (the maximum ever shown) the earliest (to date) must be the Lenormant relief at Athens (Fig. 15), probably of about 400 BC (a further, similar fragment of relief can be seen in Italy). Three-level ships last until AD 323, the last occasion on which they are named specifically as being in service, and after which they disappear for ever from history. These are, of course, the triremes.

The monoreme ship, with one man per oar, all sat at the same level in a line along each side of the ship, one behind the other, provided a basic layout . To add more power for speed and/or endurance, additional pairs of rowers were included until, at twenty-five per side, the resulting ship, as we have seen, was too long and thin and became very weak structurally as well as unmanoeuvrable. As far as illustrated sources tell us, the greatest number is in fact twenty-two per side, a 'twenty-two-er' (Fig. 9 and others).

To increase power beyond this limit imposed by the monoreme layout meant trying to pack more oars into the same hull length, and to do so a second set of rowers was added, seated slightly above and outboard of the first and utilising the gaps between them. Thus the number of rowers and rowing power could be doubled in the same length of hull, more than offsetting the increase in cross-section of the hull needed to accommodate them. This had the added benefit of contributing to better strength and seaworthiness for the ship. The benefits seem to have been applied mostly in accommodating the same twenty-five or so rowers on each side in a shorter, more handy hull. Confusingly and harking back to an earlier topic, it seems that ancient writers made no distinction between monoreme and bireme ships, referring to both as 'penteconters'.[30]

The next and final logical step to further increase power and with it to introduce bigger and more powerful ships, was to add a third set of rowers, above and outboard once more of the other two. In order to maintain the same gearing for these topmost oars, their tholes were mounted on an outrigger, which was supported by brackets projecting beyond the side of the hull on each side. This interpretation of the trireme is now the generally accepted one, especially since the building and successful operation of the *Olympias*.[31] Up to then a debate had fairly raged as to how a trireme was operated and there are still dissenting views.[32]

The lowest level of rowers were called by the Greeks thalamites (*thranetes*), after the *thalamos* (cabin, cubicle or, here, the side of the hull) in which they sat; next up were the zygites (*zygetes*), after the *zygos* (thwart or beam going from side to side across the hull) on which they sat; finally, the topmost level sat level with and adjacent to the top wale of the hull, or *thranos*, and were thus called the thranites (*thranetes*). All three of these terms are admittedly here used in their Anglicised versions; nevertheless, only these three classes of rowers and no others were ever mentioned or have been shown to have existed in the ancient world.

Following on from the trireme, warships continued to grow in 'numbering' and in size. Two men per oar in an enlarged bireme produced the quadrireme or 'four'; however, the same result would be obtained by having two men to one oar (double banking) in one of the tiers of a trireme, or even four men per oar in a big monoreme: nothing should be excluded without hard evidence. In the case of the quadrireme, almost uniquely, there is at least some evidence, in the shape of a surviving inscription from Rhodes listing the complement of such a ship (see Chapter 5). As both thranite and zygite rowers are separately specified, it can be concluded with some certainty that the ship was a bireme. Doubling up the rowers in the top two remes of an enlarged trireme produced the quinquereme or 'five'; or perhaps a bireme arrangement, with three men on, say, the upper oar and two on the lower oar of the group and so on (Fig. 16).

The Hellenistic naval powers of the eastern Mediterranean carried on a naval arms race in the third and second centuries BC, which gave rise to ever-increasing numbers and to the growth of monster ships or polyremes, the 'sixteen' already met being exceeded by Ptolemy's 'twenty', two 'thirties' and a freak 'forty'. Lesser ships, in the eight to thirteen range, were quite commonly built and used in some numbers.[33] How the oar systems of such ships were arranged is unknown and open to conjecture, but, with the known limit of three horizontal levels and accepting the Renaissance limit of eight men to an oar,[34] theoretically any arrangement up to a 'twenty-four' is possible in any of several configurations.

In interpreting Roman warships, fortunately, consideration of these more esoteric forms are not required, as the largest configuration known to have been employed in regular service by the Roman Navy was a 'six', which could therefore be a monoreme with six men to an oar, a bireme with three men to each of two oars or a trireme with two men to each of three oars and so on.[35]

This leads to a further point about multi-level rowing systems, namely their relative power. One man per oar will contribute, not surprisingly, one 'manpower' to the operation of that oar and thus the propulsive power of the ship as a whole. Placing two men

Figure 13. Above, extract from a tomb painting at Saqqara, *c.* 2500 BC; below, extract from a wall painting at Thera, Santorini, *c.* 1650 BC.

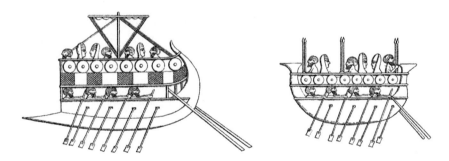

Figure 14. Phoenician biremes, *c.* 710 BC, with and without ram. After Torr, from Layard, showing a part of the relief since lost.

Figure 15. The Lenormant relief, showing the starboard side of a trireme accurately and in scale, *c.* 400 BC. It has been a most important key to the decipherment and reconstruction of the oar system of the ancient trireme.

Monoreme or 'conter' type. A single line of rowers sat one behind the other along each side of the ship, up to a maximum of 25 per side (a penteconter)

Doubling the rowers at each oar increased power but as the length of the oar stroke is dictated by the inboard man, the outboard man can only add 3/4 'man-power' as opposed to the bireme arrangement.

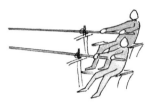

Bireme. By semi-superimposing another reme slightly outboard of the first, the ship's oarpower was doubled for little increase in length.

'Four' or quadrireme. Logical development of the bireme. By doubling the rowers at each oar in an enlarged hull.

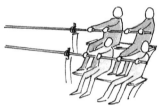

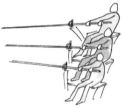

Trireme, added a third reme above and outboard of the others, their oars worked across an outrigger projecting beyond the ship's side.

The quinquereme or 'five'. By doubling the rowers per oar in the upper two remes. The standard line-of-battle ship of the Punic Wars.

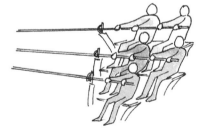

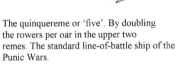

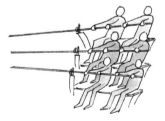

The 'six', the largest type known to have been in service with the Roman Navy.

Figure 16. Ancient rowing systems.

on the same oar does not, however, increase the power to 'two manpower'; the operation of the oar is always limited to the reach of the rower on its inboard end, which must therefore determine the length of the stroke. For a rower of an average height of, say, 5 feet 6 inches (1.68m), on a fixed seat, over an extended period at a moderate, cruising speed rate of say ten strokes to the minute, a reach of about 3 feet 6 inches (1.06m) is reasonable; for a sprint in battle, the stroke rate could be more than doubled and the reach increased by twelve inches (305mm) or so, but only for a very short period before tiring.[36] The extra man outboard of the rower will therefore work his section of the oar loom for a lesser part of its arc, which diminishes the closer he gets to the thole pin. So, if the inboard man pulls through 3 feet 6 inches (1.06m) of arc, the next man to him outboard will manage to pull through 2 feet 9 inches (840mm) of the arc and a third man outboard of him, in turn, through only 2 feet of the arc (610mm). Let it also not be forgotten that the longer the oar, the slower the operation and striking rate.

Using the 'six' as an example, therefore, as a bireme with three men per oar on two levels and with each inboard man counting as 'one manpower', the next rower outboard of him will contribute approximately four-fifths of a manpower and the outermost rower roughly three-fifths of a manpower. Thus a total of two and two-fifths manpower per oar, times two, gives a grand total of four and four-fifths manpower for the whole six-man group. If, however, the same ship is arranged as a trireme with three horizontal levels and two men per oar, each oar will have one and four-fifths manpower, which multiplied by three makes a total of five and two-fifths manpower, over half a manpower more from the same number of rowers at no extra cost. But, with a trireme arrangement, geometry dictates that the angles at which the upper two levels have to operate in such a large ship becomes more vertical and thus less efficient (see Chapter 5). In addition, the thranite rowers are higher above the waterline, adding to top-weight.

SOME PROBLEMS OF INTERPRETATION

The foregoing is an account of what might be considered the generally accepted solution to the problem of how ancient rowing systems worked. However, in the later medieval and Renaissance periods, another great age of oar-powered warships in the Mediterranean, the ships were all rowed at a single level, great and small alike, and normally by two or three men to a single oar-bench, each pulling a closely horizontally spaced oar. This was facilitated by canting the oarsmen's bench towards the stern at its midships end. This system was called *alla sensile*, and the Venetians found that five men/oars was the maximum to which this arrangement could be enlarged. The alternate system and that which superseded the former was to have one massive oar or sweep, pulled by several men, a system called *a scaloccio*. Up to eight men per oar was the maximum found to be practical. It was also found that the three one-man oars of the former system were more efficient than one three-man oar of the latter, and in fact it needed four men per oar to equal the power of three men rowing *alla sensile*, proving, if such were necessary, the contention in the last section.

The advantage of the latter was that only the inboard man needed to be trained and the layout was simpler in the *scaloccio* system (Fig. 17).[37] It is generally held that these systems have no relationship at all to the rowing methods of ancient warships. However, if we consider the spacing of the oar-ports on the *Victory of Samothrace* statue in the Louvre and the way that the two oars emerge en echelon on the Palazzo Spada relief and in the Palazzo Barberini mosaic (Fig. 18), what is noticeable is the way in which they show two levels of oars, very closely spaced vertically and not widely enough to comprise two distinct levels, as one would expect in a bireme. Perhaps the system was evolved to lessen the angles of operation of the oar remes, whilst maintaining maximum freeboard. Some of these and indeed others like them could be demonstrating that they were rowed *alla sensile*. Both the Barberini and Samothrace ships could be meant to represent smaller types, and indeed are generally taken to do so.[38] The paired oar-ports en echelon suggest a bireme, but shortened in vertical scale (Fig. 18). The *alla sensile* system would fit and work well with this design, although, as can be seen, it need not be necessary for the rowers to rise to deliver their stroke. The problem arises with the Spada relief, which is clearly intended to show a larger type of ship with a tower and must therefore represent a quadrireme or larger. One must also assume on a relief so meticu-lously detailed and executed that the details are correct. The *alla sensile* system with one man to each of the oars shown is obviously insufficient power for them, and some form of multiple manning must be assumed. With the oar-ports and their thole-pins[39] in the same vertical plane, however, the rowers of each upper and lower oar of a pair must be the same distance from the thole-pins or above each other, otherwise the gearing of each oar must differ. Several attempts to effect a drawing of how this could work with such close spacing of the pairs have failed, unless one is pulled and the other pushed. The problem thus presented is that pulling an oar imparts a lot more power than pushing it, giving rise to another discrepancy. This could be lessened if the 'pushers' were standing, but the introduction of pushers then will no longer accord with the horizontal spacing. A further solution attempted was to adopt two very long, closely spaced oars, each oper-ated by three men, interspersed along the same oar-bench, effectively a mixture of the two medieval systems. From midships, the first, third and fifth men operate the upper, slightly longer oar, while the second, fourth and sixth men operate the lower oar, the inboard two having to half-rise to deliver the stroke. This would work (at least on the drawing) and result in a very much simplified internal construction arrangement, with possibly a lower weight distribution. Against that, however, the use of huge oars dictates a slower striking rate and a shorter stroke with a consequently lower speed.

With such widely spread, yet consistent examples, clearly the intention to show oars emerging in this fashion was deliberate, but the closeness of the spacing of the oars leaves insufficient room for numbers of rowers on each oar: perhaps the paired oars were linked in some way and operated by a single crew – conjecture once more. Whatever means was adopted, there would have been no point in this new method unless it furnished a clear advantage. What that may have been, one can only try to guess.

Neither the Samothrace *Victory* nor the Isola Tiberina statuary Rome, similar in concept, shows any details of oar-ports or spaces for oars to emerge from under the

Rowing *alla sensile*

By aligning the rowing bench at an angle from the hull side, clearance was given for each man. All oars were the same length.

Rowing *a scaloccio*

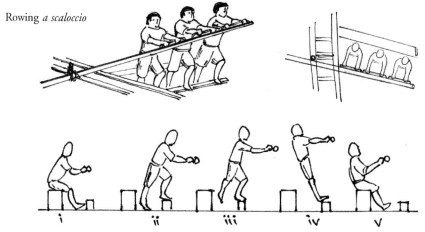

    i   ii   iii   iv   v

In the above systems, the rower had to rise to deliver the stroke from sitting (i) pushing forward and putting his foot on the foot bar, (ii) rising fully at the catch (iii) and falling back with his full weight, (iv) then returning to the original sitting position at the end of the stroke (v).

It appears that this system was known to the ancients. The illustration is from a painting in the Mastaba of Mereruka, *c.* 2330 BC and is one of several Egyptian pictures showing rowers rising to deliver the stroke; here the artist has depicted rudimentary rowing benches.

Figure 17. Medieval and Renaissance rowing systems.

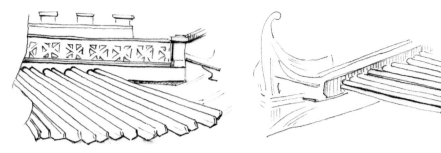

Extract from a relief showing the stern of a warship, second century AD.

Extract from a mosaic, early first century BC.

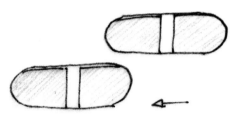

Oarports as portrayed on the Samothrace prow, early second century BC.

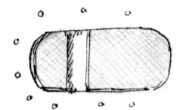

Sketch of an oar-port from Pisa ship C, including integral iron thole-pin.

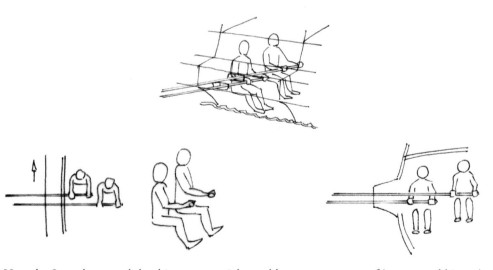

How the Samothrace and the ship at upper right could operate as a type of 'compressed bireme'.

Figure 18. Oar-port spacing *en echelon*.

outrigger, as one would expect from a multi-level system. Accordingly, the *sensile* and *scaloccio* systems ought not to be dismissed out of hand in relation to ancient ships. The ancients were capable of inventing and perfecting far more complicated systems than either of these, which surely cannot have been beyond their wit.

In support of such a consideration, the historian Polybius (*c.* 200–118 BC) describes the flagship of the Carthaginian commander as 'a single-banked[40] vessel with seven men to each oar, which had once belonged to King Pyrrhus'.[41] This was at the Battle of Mylae in 260 BC, at which time the ship would have been the best part of twenty years old (the 'Pyrrhic War' was 280–275 BC). He describes the Consular Roman flagships at the Battle of Ecnomus in 256 BC as one 'whose oars required six men apiece'.[42] Further, at the end of the war against Philip of Macedon in 197 BC, all but six ships of his navy were surrendered to the Romans. The retained ships were described by Polybius as 'five light vessels and his huge flagship in which the men rowed eight to an oar'.[43] Clearly Polybius is describing ships rowed *a scaloccio*, although it is also fair to say that he does not mention how many oars or levels of oars there were. Nevertheless, the ship was unusual enough and, indeed, unique in being described by him, and it is not an unreasonable assumption to say that if it were rowed at more than one level, he would have mentioned that as well, but it is only an assumption and one which can be called into question. This latter ship was captured by the Romans at the end of the Third Macedonian War in 167 BC and sailed by them all the way back to Rome. Polybius himself was in Rome from 166 BC and could well have seen the ship, or at least spoken to people who had done so very recently, and there is no pressing reason to doubt the accuracy of his description. However, bearing in mind what has already been discussed, in successive copyings, translations and transliterations of Polybius' work throughout Renaissance times, when only the *scaloccio* and *sensile* systems would have been known, corruption of the original text cannot be ruled out. Indeed and as an example, a more recent translation of Tacitus included the lamentable substitution of the terms 'company commander' for centurion and 'battalion' for cohort, presumably in a misguided attempt to use terms more familiar to the modern reader, but losing the real meaning in the process.

To summarise the principles involved, the whole object of the exercise is to get the maximum power per foot-length of the ship's hull, and this can only be done by increasing the number of oars and muscles operating oars, that is the number of rowers. We cannot rule out the possibility that the ancient ship designers and builders, with experience of thousands of ships over hundreds of years, tried every conceivable method and system, even including some that may well have since been lost. All of these observations and arguments will reappear later as we come to consider the interpretations that follow for each ship and the processes that led to their realisation in drawing and model form.

NOTES

1   Polybius, XVI.3.
2   For example, observe the dispute between Torr and Tarn; see Torr, *Ancient Ships* (the 1964 edition includes both sides of the dispute).
3   Homer, for example, refers to them in both his *Iliad* and *Odyssey.*
4   For example, Thucydides, *Peloponnesian Wars* I.13, avers that the first triremes were built by the Corinthians; Xenophon, *The Persian Expedition* I.4.
5   For example, Homer, *Iliad* I.309.
6   For example, Herodotus at IV.148.
7   Homer actually specifies three sizes of ship, of twenty, thirty and fifty oars; for a fifty, see *Odyssey* VIII.34; also Thucydides, I.10; Herodotus, I.152.
8   In 258 BC, in the war between Antigonos and Ptolemy, and again at the Battle of Chios in 201 BC, although she may not have been engaged at the latter.
9   Marc Antony also had tens in his fleet at Actium in 31 BC but these were old Hellenistic ships.
10 Vegetius, IV.33.
11 Having said that, there are surviving examples which have the most intricate and exquisite detail in their carving, which does not include ships, regrettably.
12 Tacitus, *The Histories* II.35.
13 Welsh, *Building the Trireme.*
14 Rodgers, *Greek and Roman Naval Warfare*, contains many drawings based on this premise.
15 Barras de la Penne, *La Science des Galères* of 1697, a manuscript now in the National Library of France.
16 Morrison, Coates and Rankov, *The Athenian Trireme.* To prove the point, extend the fingers of a hand; the longest are in the middle; close them onto the palm and the finger ends are in a straight line.
17 Rodgers, *Greek and Roman Naval Warfare*; Guilmartin, *Gunpowder and Galleys.*
18 Morrison, Coates and Rankov, *The Athenian Trireme*; the problem is also discussed at length in Morrison and Coates, *Greek and Roman Oared Warships.*
19 Morrison, Coates and Rankov, *The Athenian Trireme.*
20 Thucydides, I.93, for example.
21 Rodgers, *Greek and Roman Naval Warfare.*
22 Specialised sheds for stowing ships hauled out of the water have been identified, *inter alia*, at Piraeus, Apollonia, Marseilles and Carthage. They are mentioned by Herodotus, III.45.
23 Anderson, *Oared Fighting Ships*; Conway, *Age of the Galley.*
24 For example, the Royal Navy's Duke Class frigates, 436 × 49 feet (133 × 15m) = 8.9:1; the US Navy's Arleigh Burke class, 466 × 59 feet (142 × 18m) = 7.9:1.
25 Rodgers, *Greek and Roman Naval Warfare.*
26 Orosius, VI.19, quoted in Morrison, Coates and Rankov.
27 Polybius, XV.2.
28 Contrast Polybius, XV.2 and II.9; also Caesar, *Civil War* III.III.24 and III.V.100.
29 Reliefs from the Palace of Sennacherib at Nineveh, showing the evacuation of Tyre by Phoenician galleys in 702 BC. Examples can be seen in the British Museum.
30 Casson, *Ships and Seamanship.*
31 Morrison, Coates and Rankov, *The Athenian Trireme* and Welsh, *Building the Trireme.* Conversely, Morrison does hold that there was also a 'Phoenician' type of trireme which did not have an outrigger.
32 See Torr and the views of Tarn and others, and also Tilley, *Seafaring on the Ancient Mediterranean.*
33 Polybius, XVI.3.
34 Casson, *Ships and Seamanship.*

35 The occasional mention of use by Romans of bigger ships were of captured or requisitioned ships; there is no reference to the Romans ever building such ships.

36 Morrison, Coates and Rankov, *The Athenian Trireme* and Welsh, *Building the Trireme*; a striking rate of thirty-six to thirty-eight strokes per minute was achieved in the *Olympias*.

37 Guilmartin, *Galleons and Galleys*; Conway, *The Age of the Galley*.

38 Morrison, for example, is of the opinion that the Samothrace statue represents a trihemiolia.

39 The thole-pins are clearly represented on the Samothrace statue and their position within the oar-ports is confirmed by the excavation of an actual ship with such oar-ports, again with integral thole-pins, namely Ship C at Pisa.

40 Here the term has been misused to mean a monoreme. 'Bank' (in this context) means the number of men pulling the same oar and sitting on the same bank or bench; so 'double-banked' means two men to the same oar, 'triple-banked' means three and so on.

41 Polybius, I.23.

42 Polybius, I.26.

43 Polybius, XVIII.44.

3

SHIP FITTINGS

THE RAM

The ram was an extension of the forefoot of the hull intended to be driven into an enemy vessel to cause sufficient damage to disable it or at least to seriously compromise its ability to continue in action. Hitherto, naval warfare was simply a continuation of land battles, the only purpose of ships and boats being to bring opposing soldiery into contact with each other. The ram changed all that by making the ship itself the weapon and the enemy ship, rather than its crew, the target. Without the ship to fight from, the crew, no matter how skilful or ferocious, were just so many helpless swimmers.

Representations of ships with an extension of the forefoot of the stem at or below the waterline date from Minoan and Mycenean times (1600–1200 BC), but there is no evidence to suggest that this was a weapon (Fig. 19). Homer, writing in the eighth century BC (and therefore at a time when the ram was well established) of events thought to have taken place in the twelfth or thirteenth centuries BC, nowhere mentions naval battles or ship-to-ship combat. Although the Trojans had ships, they made no attempt to intercept or interdict the invasion fleet. The earliest known naval battle for which there is pictorial evidence of the types of ship engaged is the great battle in the Nile Delta in 1176 BC, when the fleet of Rameses III defeated that of the Sea Peoples.[1] None of the ships shown in such detail by the famous contemporary reliefs of the battle at the temple of Medinet Habu have rams or are even shown in collision. Some Minoan ships shown in wall paintings have an extension at the stern, which some have suggested is in fact the bow and a ram, with the ship being depicted going astern. This seems unlikely, as the projection hardly extends beyond the hull proper, and the same feature can still be found at the sterns of small Mediterranean craft (Fig. 20).

The explanation, it is suggested, is to be found in the evolution of rowed ships where the bow extension was found to improve the passage through the water and reduce the bow wave with its adverse effect on the forward-most rowers. This seems to have been borne out in practice.[2] Perhaps, in fact, this evolved design feature became a weapon only after an accident between two such ships demonstrated the effect that a deliberate attack could have.[3] The earliest incontestable representation of a ram appears on a bronze fibula or brooch dating from *c.* 850 BC from Athens.

Thereafter, ships with rams, which can only be of offensive intent, are commonly shown

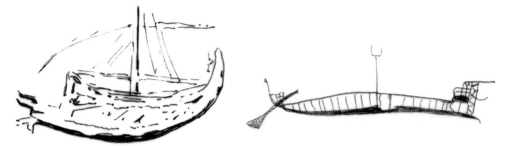

Figure 19. Examples of a forefoot on bows which do not appear to be rams. Left, Minoan *c.* 1600 BC, from a seal, after Casson. Right, Mycenean, detail of a painted clay box from Pylos *c.* 1200 BC, after Meijer.

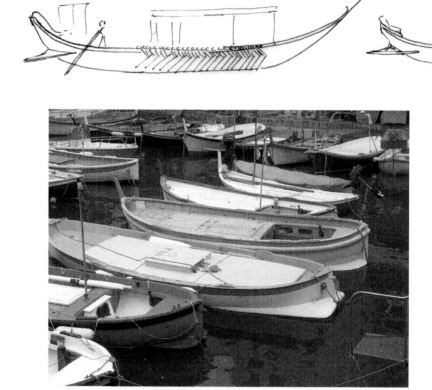

Figure 20. (Above) Minoan, sketch of a detail from a wall painting at Thera *c.* 1550 BC, showing unidentified stern projections; (below) similar projections at the sterns of modern small boats at Camogli, Italy, 2006.

on pottery, seals, coins and in stone reliefs. These early rams are pointed (Fig. 21A),[4] designed no doubt to pierce a hole in an enemy hull. The problem with this seems to have been that it was easy for the ram to become stuck when the ramming ship tried to withdraw. By the sixth century BC, therefore, Greek renditions of ships start to show the ram as a metal casting with a blunted end to punch a hole by pushing the victim's timbers inward over a wider area rather than simply trying to make a hole (Fig. 21B).[5]

The impact of a ramming attack could be as dangerous for the attacker as for the victim, so the extension of the forward hull upon which the ram was mounted had to be of heavy timbers, so placed as to distribute the force of impact back as widely as possible along the hull and for it to be absorbed, rather than concentrated, when it could cause serious damage to the attacker.[6]

The growth of ships required ever-greater castings for their rams, which in turn required more massive timbers to bear them. Even those fixings, however, were not foolproof and there are several reports of ships in ramming actions losing their rams or having them twisted off.[7] In principle, the ram was like the lizard's tail: if ensnared, the ram would break away, leaving the ship seaworthy.

In parallel with the growth and development in form of the ram went the adding of armour to oppose it. Belts of heavy timber were added along the waterline of warships, and their outriggers or sponsons for oar-mounting were reinforced by and made from stronger timbers.

The form of these later rams became more sophisticated, having a central, vertical spine and horizontal blades to cut the actual grain and joints of the shell-planking of an enemy hull (Fig. 21C).[8] This form predominated throughout the Punic Wars and, indeed, up to at least the first century AD. From the beginning of the growth towards warships larger than triremes in the fourth century BC, the primacy of ramming as a battle tactic lessened, the bigger ships being less handy and impervious, due to their armour, to ramming by smaller or even equal ships. The seaborne land battle had progressively returned, which the Romans in any event preferred. Certainly opportunities to ram arose and were taken and losses were occasioned, but more often than not it was the increasing number of marines on a ship that decided an outcome.

Later, having systematically destroyed its enemies, the Roman Navy had no opponents, and the huge rowing warship with its vast ram became an expensive obsolescence. With the end of opposing rowing navies and the advent of lighter barbarian craft, however, the ram in its adapted form would once more come into its own. The ram principle was still valid as a weapon against the newer forms of enemy that appeared, but suitably amended to attack different forms of shipping. The ships of Rome's new enemies were smaller, open craft, and the ram thus became upturned, designed to ride up and over an enemy bulwark to submerge it, rather than to pierce it, similar to a modern icebreaker that rides up onto the ice and then crushes it with its weight. This form appears in the second century AD and continues in use right up to the end of the Western Empire and beyond (Fig. 21D and E).[9]

A Phoenician, eighth century BC. Sharply pointed, sheathed in metal and intended to pierce and hole an enemy hull.

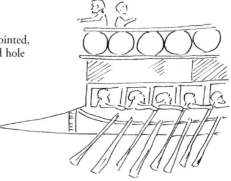

B Greek, sixth century BC. Bronze casting of a stylised animal form but with a blunt end intended to stove in an enemy hull.

C Hellenistic, fourth century BC. Highly developed as a massive bronze casting with a vertical spine to break into an enemy hull and horizontal vanes to cut the shell-planking along the grain and joints.

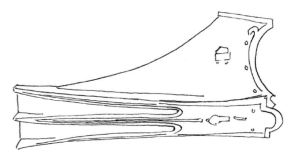

D Roman, second century AD. Unopposed by armoured hulls, this was intended to cut into light or open enemy hulls.

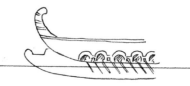

E Late Roman, fourth century AD. Not intended to puncture, but to ride up and over the bulwark of an enemy and to submerge it.

Figure 21. Evolution of the ram.

FIGUREHEADS

From the bows of warships and mounted above the ram, examples have been found of decorative bronze fittings, formed to fit over the forward ends of the wales where they meet the stempost (Fig. 22). Both examples found date from the first century BC and display quality and craftsmanship of the highest order. They are in effect the predecessors of the much later figurehead and may have had the same significance. The first example (Fig. 22A) could only be from a small warship, nothing larger than a liburnian, the trailing ends being made to fit over wales of approximately 4 by 2 inches (100 × 50mm) or so; it has a head of Minerva, the Roman goddess of war, and was possibly from a ship of that name.[10] The other set of fittings (Fig. 22B) is very much larger and would fit wales of perhaps 12 by 4 inches (305 × 100 mm), enough to suit a quinquereme. They display heads of Castor and Pollux, first adopted by the Greeks and then by the Romans as patrons of seamen and travellers at sea.[11]

A more prominent form, and one that can be accepted as a true figurehead, is the crocodile on the bow of the ship in the Praeneste relief (Fig. 51), a trireme of that same name also being known from a later tombstone. More commonly seen are devices affixed to either side of the very bows of warships. The most common are the traditional *oculus* or eye,[12] like that to be seen on the river liburnian on Trajan's Column referred to in Chapter 7. Trajan's own trireme in the same scene sports a splendid seahorse. There are others, such as the swan with its wings outstretched on the prow in Figure 66 and on the Pozzuoli triremes in Figure 67.[13]

BOARDING

For the Romans, certainly up to the third century AD and possibly later (there are no accounts), although ramming was highly desirable if opportunity presented, ultimately battles at sea were decided by boarding, so that they could use their most effective weapon, their superb infantry. Considerable ingenuity was expended in finding ways of getting their marines on to an enemy deck. From the start of the First Punic War (264–241 BC) the principal warship type used in battles was the 'five' or quinquereme; the normal complement of marines for this type was forty men, but when going into a major engagement, the Romans embarked an additional century (c. eighty men) of legionaries.

To get this overwhelming force on to an enemy ship the Romans invented a device known as the *corvus* or raven, described thus by the historian Polybius:

> A round pole about twenty-four feet (7.32m) high and ten inches (255mm) in diameter was erected on the prow of the ship. At the top of this pole was a pulley and at its base a gangway four feet (1.22m) in width and thirty-six (11m) in length made of planks which were nailed across each other. Twelve feet (3.66m) from one end of the gangway an oblong slot was cut, into which the base of the pole was fitted and each of the long

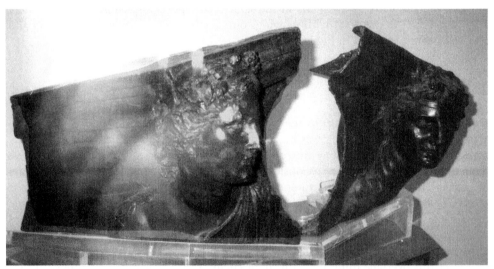

Figure 22. (Above) a smallish Roman decorative fitting in bronze, first century BC, designed to cover the forward ends of wales, where they meet the stempost. Found in the sea near Actium and possibly lost in that battle. (Photograph © the author, image reproduction for non-commercial purposes courtesy the Trustees of the British Museum.)

(Below) a much larger, similar set of fittings made in three parts (the centre piece is missing), early first century BC. Part of a merchant ship cargo from the Mahdia wreck, Tunisia.

sides of the gangway was protected by a rail as high as a man's knee. At the outboard end of the gangway was fastened an iron spike shaped like a pestle; this was pointed at one end and had a ring at the other and looked like the appliance which is used for pounding corn. A rope was passed through the ring and thence through the pulley at the top of the pole. When the ship charged an opponent, the 'raven' would be hauled up by means of the pulley and then dropped onto the deck of the enemy vessel; this could be done either over the bows, or the gangway could be swivelled round if the two ships collided broadside-on. As soon as the 'raven' was embedded in the planks of the deck and fastened the ships together, the soldiers would leap onto the enemy vessel. If the two ships were alongside, they could board from all the way down the hull, but if they had collided bows on, the men stayed on the gangway and advanced down it two abreast. The leading pair then protected their front by holding their shield before them, while the files who followed guarded their sides by resting the rims of the shields on the top of the railing.[14]

His description, although rich in detail, leaves many questions unanswered. For example, would it not have been better to have two 'raven's beaks' so that when dropped, the gangway did not rock from side to side as the men crossed? Another point is the necessity for the long slot, which surely needed only be long enough to locate one end of it at the base of the pole, but which, as described, would seem to give away up to a third of the effective length of the gangway. It would, however, enable the device to be operated with a variable length, depending upon whether a long reach was needed, for example when bridging bow-to-bow, or a shorter span if bridging beam-to-beam. Finally, he says that the ring at the end of the 'pestle' was for attaching the rope used for raising and lowering the *corvus*; this means that the marines would have to get around the rope at the very moment that they stepped on to the enemy deck, presumably opposed. Logic would suggest that rope be attached to a yoke above head-height and from which two ropes held either side of the bridge. Needless to say, there are no surviving contemporary illustrations of the device (Fig. 23).

Polybius lived between *c.* 200 and 118 BC and was present at the naval operations of the Third Punic War of 151–146 BC. At the time that he wrote, the device had been out of use for about a century, long enough for not only him but anyone to whom he could have spoken never to have seen one; nevertheless, he could also have seen written descriptions or pictorial representations long since lost to us. An interesting point that he does touch upon is that if the opposing ships come alongside, they can grapple and the men climb over along the length. The Punic strength lay in their use of the ram, and the weapon was thus intended to oppose such an attack by concentrating on bridging the gap when the two ships came into contact bow-to-bow. Possibly, therefore, to deploy the *corvus* across the bows, the stempost and bow bulwarks of the ship carrying it were removed to allow a free rein. but in so doing the sea-keeping qualities of the ship were reduced. It was amazingly successful in battle, but was also heavy, and being mounted so high and so far forward, added considerable top-weight and instability, as the loss of many ships fitted with them in storms was to testify.[15]

The *corvus* was removed and taken out of service by about 250 BC and replaced by a 'boarding bridge', of which no descriptions survive, although Vegetius, writing in the

Figure 23. The *corvus*. Author's scale model of a *corvus*, following Polybius' description and mounted on a warship bow, the stempost and bulwarks of which are deleted forward to allow the *corvus* to be deployed from beam to beam. Left: raised position; right: lowered for attack.

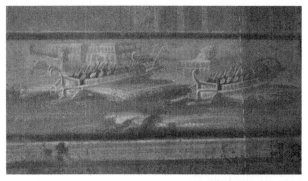

Figure 24. Wall paintings of warships showing the gap in the bulwarks (first century AD). Left: from the Temple of Isis at Pompeii; right: from the Suburban Baths at Pompeii.

Figure 25. Details from wall paintings from the Temple of Isis at Pompeii (first century AD) showing what appear to be projections alongside the stempost which may be intended to indicate boarding bridges or gangways rigged and slung outboard.

late fourth century, does say 'move out their warships alongside, throw out bridges and cross over to the enemy's ships to fight it out'.[16] It was clearly lighter than the *corvus* and could be dismantled when not required, so avoiding the problem of added top-weight, yet it could still be rigged and slung either side and marines could cross by it just as effectively. Given that the Romans continued to board and wreak havoc on enemy ships, there are clues in the iconography as to the probable form of this 'corvus replacement'. In many of the representations of warships, there appears a gap or break in the bulwark forward, just ahead of the forward end of the oar-box on each side of the ship (Fig. 24). The positioning is approximately equivalent to where a *corvus* would have been mounted, and so it seems that grapnels were thrown instead and used to pull the victim in and, when close enough, the boarding bridge would have been dropped. This takes no account of the emphasis previously placed on bow-to-bow encounters, and perhaps in practice this was not found to matter, or perhaps they had a different way of rigging it across the bows if needed, which did not require prior removal of the bow bulwarks. As to the form of the 'bridge', some curious projections shown at the forward ends of only some of the ship paintings from Pompeii (Fig. 25) could possibly represent it. Note, however, that this appears only on ships of the presumed larger type (see below) shown going away from the viewer and can hardly be considered conclusive.

The next development was introduced by Octavius' (later Augustus) admiral Agrippa during the Civil Wars of the thirties BC. Called a *harpax* (harpoon), it was a special type of grapnel having a shaft 7½ feet long (2.3m),[17] lined with metal strips so that it could not be cut through[18] and it was shot from a catapult, trailing a hawser, which was then winched in. This would require a larger type of catapult, larger perhaps than the standard 2-cubit machine which could shoot a 3-foot (0.9m) arrow and had a stock some 6 feet in length (1.7m).[19] Presumably, because of the grapnel end of the missile, it would have had to be loaded from the outboard of the catapult springs, rather than from the 'breech' end like a normal arrow or stone shot and further, the grapnel would overhang the machine. The normal arrow range for a 2-cubit machine was in the order of 400 yards (366m),[20] allowing for the added weight of the *harpax* and the line that it towed, so even if the catapult range was reduced by three-quarters, it would still be a lot further than the grapnel could have been thrown by hand.

TOWERS

Siege towers had been mounted on stationary ships by Alexander the Great for his siege of Tyre in 332 BC, but this was an extension of land-siege works and static. The first use of towers on seagoing warships and as an offensive device in battle was by the Romans. The beginning of the First Punic War saw the construction and mounting of towers aboard Roman quinqueremes, presumably as a permanent and fairly hefty fixture.[21] They were built of timber and covered by canvas, which by the Civil Wars period was painted to resemble masonry.[22] With the top-weight and wind-drag of towers added to that of the *corvus*, it is little wonder that so many ships came to grief in storms. Once again, as with the *corvus*, ingenuity was applied and an alternative form of tower brought into service by Agrippa which was collapsible and could be laid flat on deck when not in use, to keep top-weight down.[23] Towers continued in use up to the demise of the bigger galleys in the third century AD. Their size meant that towers could be mounted only on the larger ships, a 'four' or quadrireme appearing to be the smallest to mount them.

Towers could be mounted forward (Fig. 26A) or aft (Fig. 26B) and on the largest ships, probably both. They also appear singly mounted amidships (Fig. 26C) and could be mounted square to the centreline (Fig. 26A) or diagonally to it (Fig. 26B). Up to six archers and/or javelinmen could be placed in a tower but not artillery.[24] Firstly, there was insufficient working room; secondly, the shock of discharge would strain the light structure too much; and thirdly and fatally, catapults could not, because of the design of their mountings, be depressed to shoot downward on to an enemy deck,[25] something that archers could do with great rapidity. Shortly after the First Punic War, defensive

A Prow of a warship with a tower mounted well forward and square on to the hull. It is shown surmounted by a roof structure, which is thus presumably permanent, rather than the lightweight, collapsible type. Etruscan funerary urn from Volterra, second century BC.

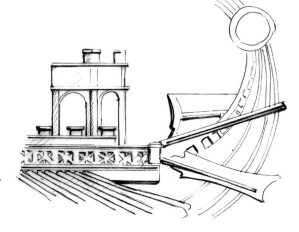

B Detail of a second-century AD relief showing a tower mounted aft and diagonally to the centreline. Original relief in the Palazzo Spada, Rome. After Anderson.

C Detail from a wall painting in the House of the Corinthian Atrium, Herculaneum, first century AD, showing ships at sea, each with a tower mounted amidships.

Figure 26. Towers.

towers were mounted on a unique and huge Syracusan merchant ship but this seems to have been the only time that they were recorded on a merchantman.[26]

One curiosity in relation to towers is the way that they are occasionally portrayed with what appear to be roofs. Figure 26A shows this as do images J and O in Figure 40. There is also the trireme on the right in Figure 67 below, but in view of its relative size, this has been interpreted as an artillery piece. One cannot conceive a reason for a roof on such towers, and as only very few of them are shown with this apparent addition, it can only be put down to some artistic or stylistic foible, however unsatisfactory such a dismissive explanation may be.

ARTILLERY

The first artillery pieces appeared at Syracuse in about 400 BC and took the form of giant composite bows, mounted horizontally and drawn by a windlass (Fig. 27A).[27] The composite bow was a wooden bow-stave, with a layer of animal sinew bonded to the outside and a layer of bone bonded to the inside of the curve of the bow. The sinew worked to contract and the bone reacted against being compressed, and these natural powers, forced into a bow by stringing and drawing, made for a powerful weapon. Applied in larger form as artillery, they could hurl a large arrow or, with suitable modification, a stone shot about 300 yards (274m). Reliable and needing little maintenance, they remained in use until *c.* 240 BC.

From about 340 BC catapults were developed, powered by stretched and twisted ropes of animal sinew or hair (the latter not so powerful).[28] These 'torsion-spring' machines were more powerful and made in many sizes up to huge versions for use in siege work (Fig. 27B). These machines were capable of shooting an arrow up to 400 yards (366m) but needed to have the cords dismounted, restretched and oiled at regular intervals. From *c.* 275 BC, formulae were perfected which dictated the relative size of each component of the catapult as multiples of the size of the holes in their frame through which the springs passed and which was one ninth of the length of the arrow the catapult was to shoot.[29] 'Formula' machines, whose range was over 400 yards (366m), were of known performance and increased reliability and could thus be mass produced.

Sizes became standardised, and for shipboard use, 3-span (shooting an arrow of 27 inches/685mm) with a stock length of 4½ feet (1.27m) and 2-cubit (a 3-foot arrow/915mm) with a stock 6 feet long (1.83m) models would appear to be appropriate. The machines could, with suitably adapted bowstrings, throw stone shot, and the larger examples could throw the *harpax*. A more difficult question is the extent of the use of fiery projectiles. Blazing 'bombs' hurled by stone throwers in siege warfare had long been in use, and special incendiary arrows had been employed, for example by the Dictator Sulla at his siege of Pompeii in 89 BC.[30] On wooden ships, anything ablaze represented a serious risk. Cooking facilities may or may not have been installed in warships, it is not known, but in merchant ships they were small and carefully lined with tile or brick.[31] There are no references to the use of fire missiles in the Punic Wars, or indeed

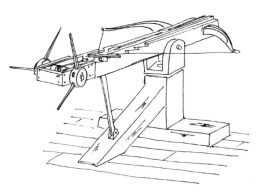

A Large arrow- and stone-throwing machines using composite bows for power, in use from 399 BC. Cocked by using a winch to pull back the slider and locking the string in a trigger mechanism. Range up to 300 yards (274m) and mounted on a universal bracket to allow elevation and traverse for aiming (with the back prop removed). Such machines remained in use down to *c.* 240 BC.

B Torsion spring-powered artillery, introduced from *c.* 340 BC, using springs of stretched and twisted animal sinew for power. Here an impression of a smaller example mounted at a ship's rail.

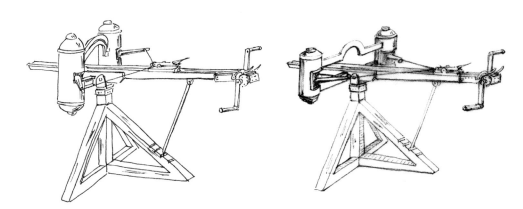

C All-metal-frame catapults with iron frames and bronze protective covers for the spring assemblies, second century AD. Range 500 yards (457m) and based on the type most commonly shown on Trajan's Column, which would suggest a mass-produced, standard type in widespread use, including the Navy. On the left, the more traditional interpretation, whereas more recent research and experiment would suggest a version with the bow-arms inward, as shown on the right.

Figure 27. Artillery.

Figure 28. Damaged stela from Salona, of a merchant ship, second century AD. The ship is in full sail with a supparum rigged above the main yard and sail. Shrouds for the mainmast can be seen, and the ship carries an artemon forward, also with sail but no standing rigging for it.

Figure 29. Detail of a stela from the Puteoli area, showing a merchant ship with halliards hanging down and the mainsail brailed up nearly to the yard. Probably early Empire.

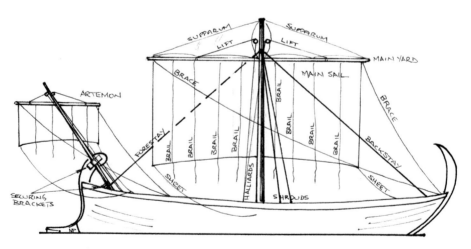

Figure 30. Warship rig; standing and running rigging.

prior to the Battle of Actium in 31 BC. In the final stages of that battle, Agrippa's ships 'shot blazing missiles and with engines threw pots of flaming charcoal and pitch'.[32] In the second century BC the Rhodians had used, to good effect, fire braziers held out on long poles to ward off enemies,[33] but this was a passive device not otherwise reported and not adopted by the Romans.

In the later first century AD, a radical design change took place, and new types of catapult were introduced, constructed with all-metal mountings for their torsion springs. They were more complex to make but more compact and powerful, as well as reliable and with a range increased to some 500 yards (457m).[34] They were again made in various sizes, the smaller being used mounted on light carriages and on the ships which had been too small for the earlier types (Fig. 27C). The articulated crank handle had been used on Caligula's ships from Lake Nemi (see below) and its use for drawing catapults, among other things, is too obvious and can be inferred from then onwards.

SAILING AND RIG

Roman warships are rarely shown under sail, but it seems reasonable to assume that all were fitted to carry a sailing rig which could be dropped and stowed when not required, or even dumped ashore to clear the decks before a battle, given enough notice. There are surviving accounts of warships landing their sailing gear prior to an action.[35] Of necessity, therefore, the rig was kept simple, so that it could be quickly set up or taken down. The primary motive power of the warship was always the oars and the rig an auxiliary for use in favourable wind conditions to rest or supplement the rowers, rather than to replace them.

Warship rig appears in only one form, namely a mainmast, mounted slightly forward of amidships, carrying a single, long yard, to which was bent a large, rectangular mainsail. The Romans did use additional triangular sails, rigged above the yard and to the top of the mast and known as a supparum (Fig. 28), but none is shown on surviving pictures of warships; although there is no reason why they should not have been so used. The mast had fore and back stays, and shrouds certainly appear by the second century AD (Fig. 29).[36] Sails were shortened or furled by means of brails or buntlines, lines that went from behind, up over the top of the sail and through rings down the front of it or 'bunt', secured at the bottom edge and working like a 'Roman' window blind when pulled (Fig. 30). The system was very ancient but robust and efficient, as sail could be taken in from the deck without having to send men aloft.

Sheets and braces controlled the bottom corners of the sail and ends of the yard respectively and apart from halliards to haul the yard and sail up to the masthead, nothing further was needed. As well as the mainmast, a foremast was also fitted, at least to the larger ships and perhaps smaller ones also for longer voyages. This was mounted in the very bows and raked forward, so that its sail was ahead of the bow, a cross between a foremast and a bowsprit. It carried a smaller, rectangular sail, square-rigged from a yard. This arrangement was known as an artemon,[37] although it is not clear whether

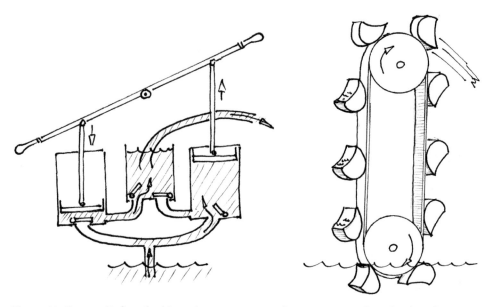

Figure 31. Pumps. Left: a double-acting pump, second century BC; right: a bucket-chain pump, first century AD.

this term applied to the mast, the sail or to the whole arrangement. This 'foremast' was secured by a deck mounting and a bracket attached to the stempost (as shown on the Praeneste relief, see below) and no standing rigging seems to have augmented this. The running rigging to operate the foresail was similar to that of the mainsail (Fig. 28).

To climb the mast, several renditions of some merchant types show steps attached to either side of the mast, or a ladder secured to the aft side of it. Ratlines seem to first appear in the fifth century AD (see military transport, in Chapter 8, below).

PUMPS

In about 148 BC, an efficient double-acting pump was developed, which, by an ingenious arrangement of chambers and valves, enabled water to be pumped on both the up and down strokes of the operating handle (Fig. 31A).[38]

The famous and huge pleasure ships built for the Emperor Gaius (Caligula, AD 37–41) and recovered from Lake Nemi had a bucket-chain form of bilge pump worked by crank handles. A chain of buckets were joined in a loop, one end revolving about a drum in the bilge of the ship to fill them and the other around another drum on the deck above, where they emptied into a chute which led over the side (Fig. 31B).[39]

PLATE I. Roman warships at sea. Two wall paintings still in situ in the House of the Corinthian Atrium at Herculaneum. The upper picture shows three ships in formation, with midships-mounted single towers. The lower painting has five ships of similar type. They are all interpreted as quadriremes (see Chapter 5). The photographs have been modified to reduce the effect of damage to the plaster backing of the originals.

PLATE II. Model of an Etruscan monoreme warship of twenty oars, suitable for the coastal waters around the Tyrrhenian Sea. See Chapter 4.

PLATE III. Half-model of a Greek-style penteconter, a monoreme of twenty-five oars per side. This ship has a flying deck amidships for access between the bow and stern and to enable the deck crew to handle the rig, which they are doing on the model. The space below had been used for stowage, including two large water jars. See Chapter 4.

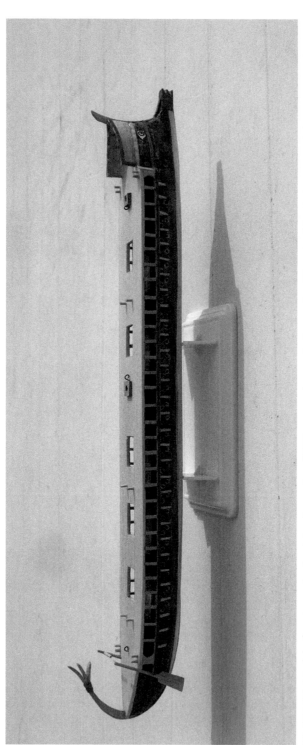

PLATE IV. Model of a trireme in the Athenian style, of 170 oars and very similar to the *Olympias*. No rig is mounted, but steps can be seen to locate the mast feet. The open gallery by the thranite oarsmen can be seen and a bulwark has been added forward to give some protection to the marines and foredeck crew. See Chapter 4.

PLATE V. Model of a *sexteres* at sea in full combat mode. The decks are packed with marines, archers, eight artillery pieces and deck crew. There are 178 figures on deck, with another 360 rowers (out of sight) below. The sailing rig has been lowered and stowed on crutches. It can be readily seen that these ships were floating fortresses, capable of overwhelming anything that they might come into contact with. See Chapter 5.

PLATE VI. Model of a quinquereme of the later type. The ship is hove-to and an eight-oar *celox* is alongside. The gangway has been lowered for the praefect and his adjutant to come aboard. The rowers (296 of them) have their oars raised and the side rudders have also been raised. The ship has four artillery pieces on deck, together with twenty sailors, the normal complement of forty marines and eight officers. For a battle, an extra century of eighty soldiers would be embarked. Although the *corvus* has been dispensed with, the much lighter boarding bridge is aboard and stowed flat on the deck forward. See Chapter 5.

PLATE VII. Model of a quadrireme from a much-modified plastic kit. The ship is equipped with a tower forward and a boarding bridge, stowed across the forward deck. The ship is shown fully rigged, with sails furled. The lower photograph is of the battery of four, 2-cubit catapults, mounted in the waist, each capable of shooting a 36-inch (915mm) bolt with a range of up to 400 yards (365.7m). See Chapter 5.

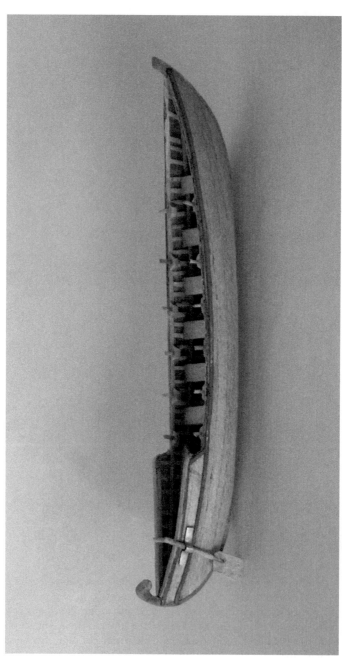

PLATE VIII. Model of a *celox* of twelve oars, the largest of the type recorded. The reconstruction is purely from the very limited description that survives and is an attempt to realise the type, based upon observation of surviving iconography of small craft generally. See Chapter 5.

PLATE IX. Wall painting from the Temple of Isis at Pompeii, showing two warships in the harbour mouth, presumably of Misenum, just across the Bay of Naples from Pompeii. The two ships are similar in appearance and both have decks crowded with marines. They obviously have more than one reme of oars, but it is not clear whether they are biremes or triremes. They are impressionistic in style and execution, as evidenced for example by the exotic sternpost decoration.

PLATE X. Model of a trireme based upon two reliefs from Pozzuoli, ancient Puteoli. The ship no longer has the gaps in the forward bulwark for a boarding bridge, but is equipped with a catapult on the foredeck. With the start of the Imperial period and demise of the big ship types, the trireme appears to have become a mainstay of the navy. See Chapter 6.

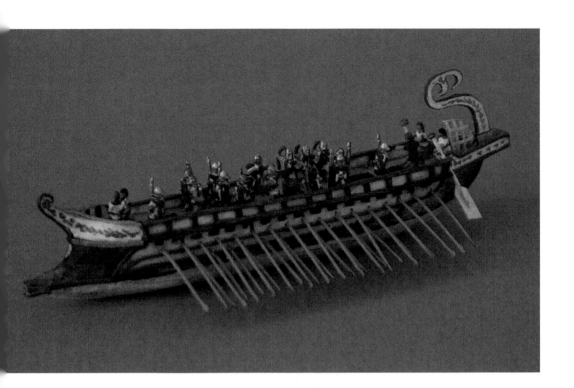

PLATE XI. Early Imperial period liburnians. Broadly based upon the wall paintings from Pompeii, the upper model is of a somewhat ornate version of this bireme warship type. In the lower photograph, two more ships of the same class are escorting a *sexteres*. Both have their sailing rig stowed on crutches and are less ornate. See Chapter 6. All of theses examples have a stern deck with surrounding screening, as opposed to the 'closed-in' stern style of the big ship, as discussed in Chapter 6.

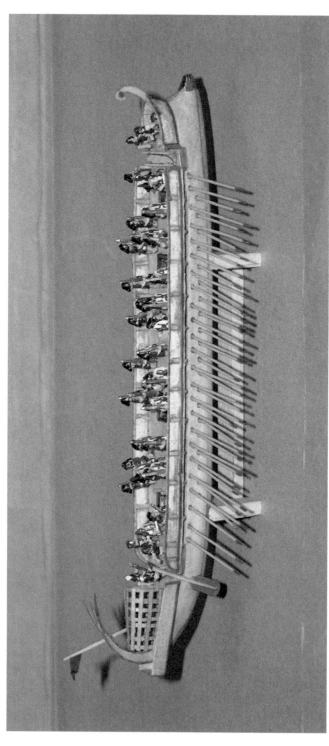

PLATE XII. An alternative interpretation of the wall paintings from Pompeii, in an attempt to produce a larger bireme warship, of reasonable dimensions. The ship is longer than the 'liburnians' previously described, with a view towards being more seaworthy, yet still conforming to the pictures, some of which do show the very short ram of this model. See Chapter 6.

PLATE XIII. Model of a small scout ship, ready for launching, with the crew on parade. The crew comprises a junior officer, perhaps a sub-optio, a helmsman, a leading hand or petty officer and twenty rowers. Each man has a pack of helmet, sword, mess tin, cloak and seat cushion, as well as a bag with provisions. The ship has two large terracotta water containers and rig stowed on crutches. See Chapter 6.

PLATE XIV. Small craft. The topmost model is the small boat illustrated in the lower drawing (Plan 18) in Chapter 6. The centre and lower models are of the boats illustrated in Chapter 7 (Plan 23). They are intended to show typical small craft of the time, which could act as tenders to bigger ships and be of a type issued to and carried by the larger warships.

PLATE XV. A bronze figurehead from the bow of a small warship, found in the sea off and at or near to the site of the Battle of Actium (31 BC). The side pieces are fashioned to fit over the forward ends of the wales where they meet the stempost, with the central boss and figure astride it and projecting forward. See Chapter 3. (Photograph © the author, image reproduction for non-commercial purposes courtesy the Trustees of the British Museum.)

PLATE XVI. A ram and stempost in marble at Ostia Antica. The stempost is slightly forward of its proper position in relation to the ram, which is approximately 2 feet (610mm) square across the fore end. The horizontal and vertical vanes for cutting into an enemy hull are clearly seen. See Chapter 3.

PLATE XVII. Model of a river-type liburnian as discussed in Chapter 8 and based upon the reliefs on the columns of Trajan and Marcus Aurelius in Rome.

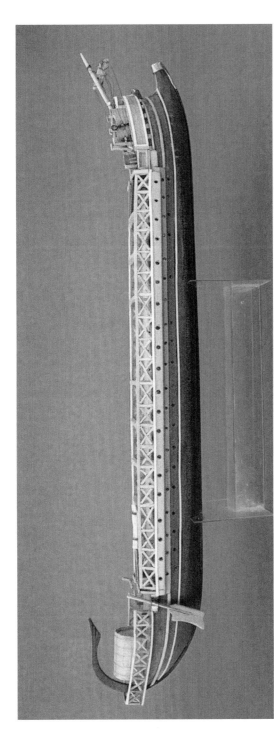

PLATE XVIII. Trajan's trireme. Model of a trireme after that shown on Trajan's Column transporting the Emperor himself. The ship follows the fashion of its smaller companions in having an open, undecked centre section over the rowers, which can be closed by awnings or covers drawn across the frames above them. The forecastle is now the principal fighting platform of the ship. See Chapter 7.

PLATE XIX. Model of the 'universal-type' military transport shown on the Columns of Trajan and Marcus Aurelius as general transports, freight carriers and pontoons. See Chapter 7.

PLATE XX. Diorama of patrol ships on the Rhine or one of its tributaries, *c.* AD 250–300, after a stone monument from Germany. These are intended to represent the larger warships of the river fleet, used to patrol the main channels and to support the lighter, open craft. See Chapter 8.

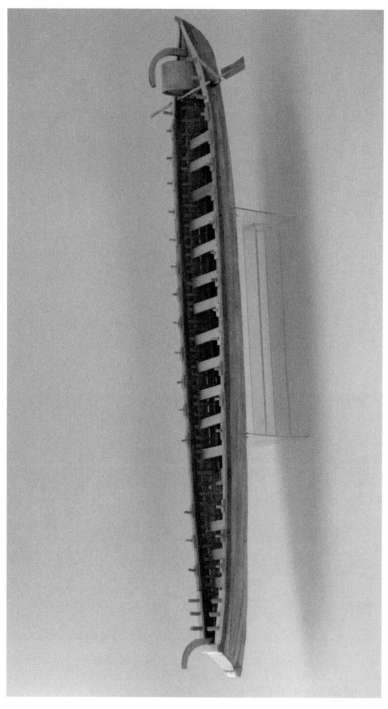

PLATE XXI. A *lusoria*, modelled on the boats recovered from the Rhine at Mainz (Moguntiacum), the former capital of the province of Upper Germany (Germania Superior) and a legionary headquarters. This is intended to represent the smaller, lighter type of river warship as posited in the text. See Chapter 8.

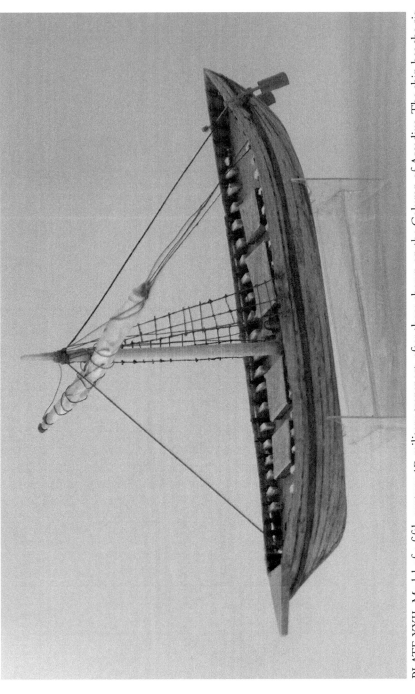

PLATE XXII. Model of a fifth-century AD military transport, after those shown on the Column of Arcadius. The ship has the rig permanently mounted and the shrouds have ratlines. Temporary oar benches have been installed to enable the ship to be rowed, otherwise the deck is dominated by the large cargo-handling hatches. See Chapter 8.

PLATE XXIII. An interpretation of how one of the last of the Western Empire's warships may have appeared. It is totally different from the warships of the earlier Empire and can be seen as the lineal ancestor of the later *dromon* of the continuing Eastern Empire. See Chapter 8.

PLATE XXIV. Details from second- or third-century AD mosaics from North Africa, the upper with the very commonly found scene of Odysseus and the Sirens, the lower with Bacchus and his acolytes. Both demonstrate the convention of showing figures oversize in relation to the ships and have warships portrayed in a highly stylised way. Certain details, however, conform to other forms of iconography, such as the depiction of a cuddy in the stern of each and the rig on the upper ship. Also noteworthy is the highly decorative painting of the hulls.

PLATE XXV. The *Olympias*, the reproduction of a fifth-century BC Athenian trireme. The top view shows the ram, the ship's principal weapon and also the reinforced front ends of the oar outrigger. In the centre is an overall view. The lower left view shows details of the mounting of the starboard steering oar, while that on the right shows the three distinct levels of oars, together with the *askomata* for the lowest (thalamite) reme.

ANCHORS

Warships were equipped with anchors, as shown by surviving records of the Athenian Navy,[40] and are known to have been used on Roman warships from ancient accounts which relate to occasions when anchors were used, commonly when mooring onto shores.[41] The type and numbers of anchors carried by Roman warships and for each type of ship is unknown, although merchant ships were known to have carried several anchors of varying sizes.[42] Metal chains were known[43] but for warships, rope anchor cables were included in the records (Athenian again) of their inventories, chain being presumably an unnecessary weight. Further, warships being very much lighter than, say, a fully laden merchantman; lighter anchors were sufficient for all but the very largest.[44] As far as stowage of anchors is concerned, neither catheads from which they would be slung nor any anchors can be identified from the iconography. Smaller ships could be hauled up on to a suitable shore, stern-first (ram-first would obviously be embarrassing); had they first dropped anchors, they could be subsequently easily hauled back off again. Other ships moored offshore were also held in position by anchors.

Anchors took several forms, the most common having a wooden shaft and arms, tipped with metal flukes and with a cast lead stock on the shaft. These were made in various sizes, and some were very large indeed. Stocks could also be of stone. Another type was wholly of iron and very similar in appearance to the (very much) later 'Admiralty' type, still in general use. Some even had removable stock-pieces exactly like their modern counterparts. These again could be very large, one second-century AD example which has been recovered being about 12 feet (4m) in length (Fig. 32).

HATCHES AND VENTILATION

Protecting the rowers in an armoured box below the decks of ancient warships solved one problem, their vulnerability to missiles, but exacerbated another, namely a lack of ventilation. Several hundred men engaged in hard manual labour in a confined, closed space for hours on end, especially if the weather was hot, would sweat profusely and soon feel the effect of a lack of fresh air.[45] The provision of adequate openings for the circulation of air was of paramount importance. Those same men also had to be able to get aboard to man their oars and also to get out quickly, especially if their ship were damaged and settling in the water. Although, once again, there are no contemporary illustrations, one can infer that these warships had a lot of large deck hatches; these could be closed by covers in stormy weather (perhaps elevated above the coamings to allow some airflow) and in action the openings could be closed by leather or wooden screens to prevent the ingress of missiles. This last would coincide with the need for the rowers to be making their maximum effort, rowing at top speed to attack or take avoiding action. Clearly 'battening down the hatches' was only done at the last minute when coming under fire and undone at every opportunity.

Figure 32. Examples of Roman anchors. Left above: a simple stone type, used from the earliest times; below: some cast lead anchor stocks, with a reconstruction in the background; the longest stock is approximately 4 feet 6 inches (1370mm) long. Right: a cast-iron 'admiralty' type, some 12 feet (4m) in length.

Figure 33. Detail of a wall painting in the Suburban Baths, Pompeii (first century AD). Between the deck-edge bulwark and the level where the oars emerge is a clearly defined horizontal course or level with vertical struts and shadowing shown to suggest an open gallery arrangement as a ventilation course for the rowers.

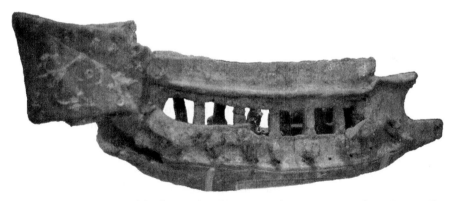

Figure 34. Terracotta model of a warship from a wreck near Cape Maleas, Greece, first century BC to first century AD, clearly showing a 'gallery' above the topmost oars, allowing ventilation below decks.

The other feature, which is shown in several contemporary depictions (see, for example, the Lenormant relief, Fig. 15, and the Praeneste relief, Fig. 51), is what appears to be a line of hatches or openings or even grilles along the hull sides, immediately above the oars. This has been very reasonably and realistically interpreted as a 'ventilation' course (Fig. 33), forming a kind of gallery of openings along the side at the level of the topmost reme of oarsmen (the thranites).[46] A possibly clearer and unequivocal example is the open gallery along the hull sides, immediately above the topmost oars, of a terracotta model of a warship found in a wreck off Cape Maleas in Greece (Fig. 34). As they were the only ones who could see the oars, the thranites were the senior ranking and dictated the stroke of the men in the remes below them. The undersides of outriggers, where fitted, could also be left open to add to the airflow and, unlike the hull-side ventilation courses and deck hatches, need not have been covered in action.

RUDDERS

Steering for the vast majority of ships up to about the twelfth century AD was by means of one or two large steering oars or side rudders, mounted on the stern quarters and operated by tiller arms, fixed at right angles to the rudder shaft, with blade surfaces both fore and aft of the shaft. They were in effect balanced rudders and by surviving accounts, a well set-up ship was light to steer.[47] The single, stern-mounted rudder was known, and there are many depictions of ancient Egyptian boats rigged with such an arrangement, slung on the stern-post and worked by a tipstaff.[48] A similar arrangement is shown on late Roman rivercraft and can still be seen on traditional Portuguese Port barges (Fig. 35A and B). There is little indication, however, that such an arrangement was developed for seagoing ships until very late, and Roman warships are almost always shown with two rudders rigged at the stern quarters. They are usually large and ornate in shape and shown emerging from the rear face of the oar-boxes built outboard of the hull proper (which forms the outrigger for the topmost oar tholes) and which is extended aft to provide rudder mountings (and protection for them). The mountings themselves, at least on smaller ships, are often shown as a metal bracket;[49] on the larger ships, they sit in a cradle and are restrained by straps, as can be seen on the *Olympias* (Fig. 35C and D). It is possible that a conventional (to us) stern-hung rudder was in use at least in the Eastern Empire by the early fifth century AD. One of a set of sixteenth-century AD drawings of the (now destroyed) Column of Arcadius (r. AD 395–408) in Constantinople appears to show ships so equipped (Fig. 88). This illustration is from a period for which there are, sadly, few surviving images of ships, and the drawings alone cannot be taken as conclusive evidence of the adoption of such a system; later illustrations of eleventh- and twelfth-century AD Byzantine ships show side rudders still used, as in earlier times (and see Chapter 8).

In relation to rudders, the Palazzo Spada relief (see Fig. 26B) is one of several that show them raised and stowed horizontally, the shafts and tillers hidden within the hull. Although the blades can be seen, no details are shown of the manner in which the

A Detail from a tomb painting showing a stern rudder operated by a tipstaff and restrained by a kicking strap. Tomb at Beni Hasan, 1991–1782 BC.

B Grave stela from Cologne, Germany, with a similar rudder arrangement; late first-century AD

C The trireme *Olympias* showing the twin steering oars or side rudders emerging from the rear of the oar-boxes (reproduction of a fifth-century BC Athenian trireme).

D Relief of a merchant ship from Salona, probably second century AD, showing an ornate port-side rudder.

Figure 35. Rudders.

rudders are pivoted or the shafts stowed or whether this impinged in any way upon the aft-most rowers.

On small ships, helmsmen are shown, usually exaggerated in size, unprotected, which seems unlikely for such an obvious target for enemy archers. On small ships, protective screens could be rigged or sailors with shields detailed to protect them, as seen in Figure 7. On the bigger ships, such as in the Palazzo Spada example, the way in which the rudders are stowed indicates a different arrangement in which the helmsmen could be below deck and thus protected. This must remain conjecture, alas.

DECK FITTINGS

Illustrations of merchant ships often show catheads forward and even bitts projecting from decks (Fig. 36), details sadly lacking from portrayals of warships (and see the section on anchors above). It can only be assumed, quite reasonably perhaps, that warships had bitts or bollards on deck for mooring, securing anchors and suchlike. For the handling of anchors and rig, larger merchant ships had 'capstans and winches on the foredeck',[50] and it is not unreasonable to suppose that the larger warships also had an anchor winch; this would in fact seem necessary to handle the larger anchors already seen. Deck rings in metal for securing stays and shrouds, together with rails for belaying pins or wooden cleats by the masts and aft to secure halliards, brails and running rigging, are simple enough to be assumed. Bronze sail rings for brails have been found in several merchant shipwrecks.

The universal arrangement for the working of oars in the ancient world was the thole-pin, a pin made from hardwood, inserted into a hole in a hardwood block or carling which was set into or affixed to the hull side at appropriate locations. The oar was held in position against the pin by a leather or rope strap, looped around both. Experience with the reproduction trireme *Olympias* showed that the oar could be worked from either the forward or aft sides of the pin (Fig. 37).[51] Recent excavation of a wreck (Ship C) at the site of the ancient harbour of Pisa has revealed oar-ports in the hull with nail holes around them to indicate where a leather *askomata* or 'glove' was secured to the hull and tied around the oar shaft to prevent the ingress of water. Most notable, however, is the integral iron thole-pin, a form which accords with and confirms the accuracy of the reliefs previously mentioned (Fig. 18).

AWNINGS

There are no surviving illustrations showing deck awnings. Caesar does, however, mention 'skins which served as awnings', thereby confirming that they were in fact used and made from leather.[52] As legionary tents were also made from leather, these must have been intended as waterproof awnings. Other awnings were, of course, known to the Romans: witness the elaborate arrangements to provide shade to the audience at

Figure 36. Stern of a merchant ship on the tomb of Eudemos at Olympos in Lycia (southern Turkey) second century BC. Two mooring bitts can be seen projecting above the stern rail. (The side rudder is removed, and a curious 'table-like' feature is shown ahead of the bitts. Could this represent a windlass?)

Figure 37. Tholes. Oars were worked around a hardwood pin inserted into a block attached to the hull side and secured by a rope strop. The system is still in use, as seen on this small rowing boat at Camogli, Italy in September 2006. For an alternative form of built-in thole, see Figure 18.

the Colosseum in Rome and at other amphitheatres such as Capua which must have been made from lighter material.[53] There is every reason to suppose that ships also could carry light weather-shade awnings, or simply perhaps rig a sail as one. Note also in this regard the midships details in Figure 33, which might well indicate awnings. As for the ships, laying off a shore, ferrying a deck-full of troops, carrying important personages or just giving some shade to a tired crew are all situations that might require the rigging of awnings, in itself a simple enough operation. As to how they may have looked, one can only refer to examples on much later galleys (Fig. 38).

Figure 38. Awnings. Renaissance galleys, showing awnings rigged over the decks to give shade. Left: detail from a painting at the Royal Palace, Caserta; right: detail from a sixteenth-century AD Maiolica tile from Naples.

Figure 39. Detail from a frieze along the stage of the theatre at Perge, Pamphylia, showing Dionysus in a boat with a gangplank leading ashore. First century AD.

GANGWAYS

When mooring alongside a quay or beam-on to a shore, no doubt the boarding bridge could be used as a gangway linking ship to shore. However, when mooring stern-on to a quay or jetty in the Mediterranean fashion, or, indeed, when ships were pulled stern-first up on to a shore, an alternative method of disembarking was used (Fig. 39). This was a gangway, one or more of which were carried by warships,[54] slung from the rear of the steering oar housing and dropped astern (see Fig. 26B). This system was, in fact, very old, and earlier Greek vase paintings frequently show ladder-like gangplanks slung over or on the sterns of ships. An identical method was used on later, Renaissance ships (Fig. 38, right).

SHIP'S BOATS

Warships, at least sometimes, carried a small boat, or *scapha* (modern Italian, *scafo*, boat or ship hull; *scafa*, long boat, lighter or tender), perhaps more than one, as a tender.[55]

There are no illustrations where a boat can be identified aboard a warship, although perhaps one of the deck structures in Figure 33 was intended to show one. Presumably they were only carried and needed by the larger ships, perhaps quadriremes and upwards. As to their form, one can only rely on the numerous examples of small boats shown in various media.

FOREDECK STRUCTURES

The earliest extant depictions of Roman warships are to be found on coins. The Romans started to issue their own money from 289 BC.[56] During the First Punic War (264–241 BC) coins started to be issued showing the prows of warships, presumably as a response to their hugely increased importance in that essentially naval war.[57] Warships remained a popular theme for coinage thereafter and well into Imperial times.

The designs of the coins during the Republican period (up to 31 BC) vary in significant respects from those of later times as well as from depictions of warships shown in other media, such as sculpture and wall paintings. In the first place, the majority of the republican designs portray only the prow of the ship, whereas a lesser number and all of the later, Imperial coins show the whole ship. Noticeably, however, the coins with prows also have considerable detail above the main deck line, which would seem to suggest some kind of structure erected on the foredecks. The small size of a coin, especially one destined for general circulation, the requirement for rapid, mass production (as opposed to the careful production of a limited number of commemorative coins) and the wear and tear of usage all go to limit a design to an overall impression only. Nevertheless,

Figure 40. Foredeck structures. (A) Republican copper *uncia*, First Punic War period; (B) similar coin; (C) bronze denarius, Second Punic War period; (D) denarius, late third/early second century BC; (E), (F), (G), (H) Republican bronze denarius; (I), (J) *denarius* of the moneyer M. Fonteius, 85 BC; (K) *as* of M. Antonius as *triumvir*, 43–31 BC; (L) similar coin; (M) denarius of Sextus Pompeius, 38 BC; (N) bronze coin of Octavian, 36 BC; (O) bronze denarius of M. Agrippa, 36–31 BC; (P) *tetradrachm* of Antigonus Poliorcetes, 306–283 BC.

over the course of the centuries the craftsmen who made the dies for these coins went to the extra trouble and effort to include these details quite deliberately on a wide variety of coins and too frequently for them to be ignored. As has been demonstrated (Fig. 7), one must start from the premise that the details show what existed.

Figure 40 is a selection of images of details extracted from photographs of various Roman coins. Images A and B are the earliest, dating from the mid-third century BC (First Punic War period). Images C, D, E, F, G, H and I are also from Republican coins of between then and the first century BC. The rest are from the first century BC, the end of the Republic. Images J, K and L are different in style, displaying a more Hellenistic influence.

The first detail to be noted is in images A, B and C, the earliest among the examples and which show long lines descending towards the bow and base of the stempost, but above the main bulwark line, with indistinct protuberances above these lines. Could these represent covers to protect the troops on deck from missiles? In support of such a contention, images D, E and F have discs that could represent crewmen's heads, which appear above the ventilation course, but beneath the superstructures (in K and L, crew heads are shown above the bulwark level, though whether they are marines on deck or rowers is not clear). Rowers would, of course, be behind and not above the ventilation course, but the vertical scale is not necessarily accurate enough, bearing in mind the constraints, to be able to distinguish accurately. Assuming that marines under protective covers are intended, do the 'protuberances' signify the *corvus*? In A and G this would seem reasonable, even B and H could be included, but C and D surely cannot be. In any event, the *corvus*, if placed as in A and G, would be too high and if dropped onto an enemy would either be fouled by its own ship or result in an extremely awkward downward-sloping ramp for the marines to try to negotiate.

The next notable item is the 'table-like' detail comprising two vertical struts and a flat top, under the 'S' over the bow of D. The same detail reappears clearly in F, H and G and recurs in more vestigial form in E and I. It is tempting to suggest that they are intended to represent towers, but the tops of them are at the same level (F, G, I and O) or only slightly higher (D, E, H and J) than the adjacent superstructure, whereas one could expect a tower to be considerably higher.

Perhaps it is intended to represent a raised platform, or even an athwartships 'bridge' for archers and slingers. In this regard, P, from a contemporary Hellenistic coin, is very different in style but having a raised platform in the bow. There are also many Hellenistic coins with ship prows without this structure. Turning to the later, first-century BC, Hellenistic-style images, image J displays a pierced, 'gallery-like' deck covering terminating forward in a low tower, the two being clearly differentiated and reflecting the earlier images, but on a different hull form. K has what appears to be a raised platform in the bow, whereas L shows a small tower crowned by an oversized pennant staff or perhaps an artemon without its yard. The image from the coin of Sextus Pompeius (M) reverts to a more traditional form of prow, but with what would appear to be prominent deck-edge rails and a curious device in the very bow, perhaps an artillery piece. There is no sign of the 'protective covering' (unless the horizontal rails are meant to show this) and none of the structures previously commented upon above, nor any tower. The contemporary counter to M is N, an early offering from Octavian, portrayed on the obverse with his adoptive father, Caesar, through whom he justified his authority. Here the ship is more finely executed, with the ventilation course and the deck and bulwark above it clearly shown, but what is intended by the prominent circular symbol and the oddly shaped symbol forward of it? Finally, image O, the latest dated, reverts to the designs of nearly two centuries earlier such as C.

Later images lessen or completely lose these details of structures on the foredecks of warships, which presumably disappeared along with the ships that mounted them, as the heyday of the larger types ended. The overall similarity in the designs between the third and first centuries BC would lead to the conclusion that the dominant type of warship of that period, the quinquereme, was the subject matter and that it was to this type that these details related, something that will be further considered (Chapter 5). In any event, without some corroboration from other media, it is not possible to draw any conclusions as to what was intended by these added details.

NOTES

1   The earliest sea battle for which a record survives was in 1210 BC between the Cypriots and the Hittites but no picture or description of the ships adjoins it.
2   Severin, *The Jason Voyage*; also the trials of the trireme *Olympias* already referred to. Similar extensions can also be found on early north European boats such as the '*Hjortspring*' boat.
3   History repeated this lesson at the Battle of Lissa in AD 1866.
4   After a relief from Nineveh; see Chapter 2, note 13.
5   From an Athenian vase.
6   See Morrison, Coates and Rankov, *The Athenian Trireme*.
7   For example the Athlit ram, fully described in Casson and Steffy, *The Athlit Ram*.
8   An example of such a ram is depicted in marble located near the Marine Gate at Ostia Antica and there is half of a cast bronze ram in the Archaeological Museum at Piraeus.
9   Examples are clearly shown on the columns of Trajan and Marcus at Rome.
10 The name is attested from grave stelae for ships of both the Imperial Misenum and Ravenna fleets.
11 Pitassi, *The Navies of Rome*.
12 There is a superb example, fashioned from thin marble sheet, in the Archaeological Museum at Piraeus, thought to have come from a trireme.
13 See also Casson, *Ships and Seamanship*.
14 Polybius, I.22.
15 Pitassi, *The Navies of Rome*; the worst was the loss of a fleet South of Sicily in 255 BC; Polybius, I.37.
16 Vegetius, IV.44.

17 Appian, *Civil Wars* V.II.8, quoted in full in Casson, *Ships and Seamanship*.

18 The Carthaginians at a battle in 202 BC had used a hand-thrown metal grapnel attached to a metal chain, so that it could not be cut; Livy, XXX.

19 Marsden, *Greek and Roman Artillery*.

20 Marsden, *Greek and Roman Artillery*.

21 Silius Italicus.

22 Pliny, *Natural History* XXXII.

23 Appian, *Civil Wars* IV.74.

24 Athenaeus, V, quoted in full in Casson, *Ships and Seamanship*.

25 Livy, XXIV.34, the Roman ships got too close for the Syracusan artillery to shoot at them; that is they got under them.

26 Athenaeus, V.206–9.

27 Marsden, *Greek and Roman Artillery*.

28 Caesar, *Civil War*, III.9; Vegetius, IV.9; *The Artillery Manual of Heron*, 111–12 (in Marsden, *Greek and Roman Artillery*).

29 Marsden, *Greek and Roman Artillery*.

30 Russo, *Assiedo a Pompeii*.

31 An example was found on the Yassi Ada wreck, a full-size replica of which is in the Bodrum Museum.

32 Dio Cassius, L.32.8.

33 Polybius, XXI.7; Livy, XXXVII.11.

34 There has been some new thinking on this subject, with very interesting new interpretations. See M. Lewis in *Current World Archaeology* no.3 and Russo, *Assedio a Pompei*.

35 Livy, XXXVI.44; Thucydides, VII.24. Conversely, at Actium, Antonius put the rig onboard as he intended to break out to the open sea.

36 See, for example, the Column of Arcadius, below.

37 The earliest depiction of a two-masted ship is Etruscan; *artemo – artemon* appears in several Latin but only one Greek text. Perhaps it was an Etruscan word?

38 Invented by one Ktesibios of Alexandria, an example has been found in the wreck of a ship; Sprague de Camp, *The Ancient Engineers*.

39 Sprague de Camp, *The Ancient Engineers*.

40 Casson, *Ships and Seamanship*.

41 Caesar mentions this in his British expeditions, *The Battle for Gaul* IV.29; see also Livy, XXV.25.

42 One of the best accounts of the use of them is the shipwreck of St Paul off Malta (Acts 27).

43 Caesar, *Gallic Wars* III.13

44 Casson, *Ships and Seamanship*.

45 Morrison and Coates, *Greek and Roman Oared Warship*, includes calculations of the amount of energy, heat and the amount of fresh air that would be required.

46 Morrison and Coates, *Greek and Roman Oared Warships*.

47 As related by Lucian in his description of the grain ship at Athens, *Navigium* 5.

48 Also Herodotus, II.96 and III.106.

49 See Trajan's Column ships and funerary urns.

50 Lucian, *Navigium* 5.

51 Morrison, Coates and Rankov, *The Athenian Trireme* and Severin, *The Jason Voyage*, for accounts of practical experience.

52 Caesar, *The Civil War* III.I.15.

53 There survives a wall painting of the amphitheatre at Pompeii showing the awnings; naval personnel were stationed at Rome to rig and operate the awnings of the Colosseum; Pitassi, *The Navies of Rome*.

54 Herodotus, IX.98; Thucydides, IV.12; Casson, *Ships and Seamanship.*
55 Livy, XXX.10; Caesar, *The Battle for Gaul* V.26.
56 Scullard, *A History of the Roman World.*
57 Pitassi, *The Navies of Rome.*

PART II
THE SHIPS

4

THE EARLIEST TYPES: EIGHTH TO FOURTH CENTURIES BC

It was to be approximately 350 years from the date of the founding of Rome (by tradition and probably not so far from fact) in 753 BC, before a Roman warship was mentioned in the surviving accounts, sailing the seas in 394 BC.[1] In the interim, Romans had embarked upon seafaring endeavours and had ships with which to do so;[2] after all, Rome's location as a trading centre was due to the River Tiber which flows through it and which was navigable then by seagoing ships of the time, up to the city itself. The first treaty between Carthage and the fledgling Roman Republic in 509 BC refers to 'the ships of Rome and her allies'.[3] These were most likely, however, to have been merchant ships, but it does confirm that Rome and the sea were no strangers.

By 394 BC, work had started on the building of quays and port facilities at the mouth of the River Tiber at what would shortly become the port of Ostia, 14 miles downstream from Rome itself. These additional facilities to connect Rome with the open sea were needed because of the increase in traffic, the growth of the size of ships and because Rome's own internal ship-handling facilities became insufficient. By this time, although the rival Etruscan sea power had been broken, the Roman coastline extended only a short way either side of and adjacent to the mouth of the Tiber, that of its allies adding little more.

As mentioned, the first account of a Roman warship was in 394 BC, when one was sent to Greece with a deputation to the Oracle at Delphi. Presumably it was not Rome's only warship, but was of a size sufficient for such a voyage and of sufficient prominence to be entrusted with such a long-range mission, with such obvious prestige attached. It was captured and later released by the locals of the Lipari Islands, off the north coast of Sicily. As the islands are small, with a correspondingly small population, unable to man large warfleets and probably using their fishing boats *en masse* to surround a potential raider, for them to have captured the warship without a fight (none is related) would seem to imply that it too was only small and not particularly fast. Indeed, it is hard to see how Rome would need, or be able, with its limited facilities of the time, to use anything more than a few coastal patrol craft to protect its fishermen and to deter the odd marauding pirate.

As to the form of such ships, at the time, the Athenian type of trireme remained queen of the battlefleets of the major maritime powers; in Syracuse and Carthage, however, the first examples of larger warships had recently appeared. Although aware of these developments, not least through their long alliance with Carthage, the Romans would have had no use for such exotic ships and can be assumed to have deployed the smaller types that would have been adequate for their limited purposes. There was little or no risk of any maritime threat, their Carthaginian ally holding the preponderance of naval power in the area, and any invasion attempt would have been met ashore by the Romans' formidable army. In any event, it is difficult to see from where any such threat might have materialised before an Adriatic seaboard was acquired.

With no attributable contemporary illustration or description, we can only assume that these ships were similar to the ships of Rome's neighbours, the Etruscans and the Greek colonies of Southern Italy (the Italiote Greeks), and it is upon this premise that the following reconstruction of these early ships is based. Rome had of course been ruled by Etruscan kings up to the beginning of the Republic in 510 BC, and the Etruscan influence was very strong. The Etruscans were a naval power themselves and their warship types and designs would have been familiar to the Romans, who probably used them, even if only by manning ships for their Etruscan overlords. When building their own first warships, they would have copied or may even have simply obtained and used Etruscan ships.

The other influence was Greek, although not initially, as the Etruscans and Italiote Greeks were violently opposed. Greek influence would have increased later, especially with the waning of Etruscan seapower and even more so after the Roman acquisition of the major Greek seaport of Naples in 326 BC. The final influence was Carthaginian, the Romans entering a succession of three maritime treaties with Carthage in 508 BC, 348 BC and 306 BC.[4] These treaties tended to be restrictive to Roman seagoing, an endeavour jealously guarded by Carthage. In the absence of surviving representations of Carthaginian ship designs, although one can assume that the Romans may have adopted some design features from them, it is impossible to identify them.

The light warship of the period was the 'conter' type, powered by anything from twenty to fifty oars, each pulled by one man at one (monoreme) or two (bireme) levels and with varying degrees of decking, from just bow and stern platforms, to 'flying' decks, to being completely decked over. There is no reason to suppose that larger biremes were not built, perhaps of sixty oars or even more. Any larger, however, and the ship becomes close in size to a trireme, against which it would have been considerably outclassed, the trireme having 170 oars in a similar-sized hull. Although it was possible to build a bireme larger than sixty oars, it would have been pointless, as one could have a trireme for virtually the same cost. By the end of this period, however, even the trireme was to lose its primacy in battlefleets.

Figure 41. Extract from an Etruscan tomb painting, sixth century BC, showing a small, open boat in use for fishing.

MONOREMES

Etruscan-style monoreme warship of twenty oars

Colour Plate II (Plan 1)

This example of an Etruscan design is developed from the elegant small boat in the painted tomb of '*caccia e pesca*' (hunting and fishing) at Tarquinia, dating from the sixth or fifth century BC (Fig. 41). The boat has the owner (the occupant of the tomb) seated in the stern sheets, holding a port-side steering oar; two others in the boat seem to be indicating 'the one that got away' across the bow, while the bow man looks to his lines. A thole-pin and oar can be made out. If this were indeed such a small boat, a side rudder would hardly be required; moreover it has a warship-style recurved bow with lee boards and a raised stempost. There is no deck sheer save for the upturned stern. If this is a pleasure-boat in the style of a warship, then enlargement, in the example to a ship of twenty oars, could reveal a monoreme, undecked conter of modest size, suitable for scouting or a little light raiding, perhaps. The bow has been 'reversed' to put the longer projection at the bottom to form a ram; a light rig can be presumed.

The building of civilian boats and ships in the fashion of warships became particularly widespread in the early Empire, especially with the development of the merchant galley, for the rapid transport of perishable goods or livestock (see Figs. 4 and 5). In this earlier period, ships would engage in trade or piracy, according to opportunity, and the difference between some merchant and more belligerent ships was not, therefore, always so clear-cut.

Other than this, it must be admitted that this reconstruction is based upon very minimal evidence for its existence, but represents an attempt to realise the light craft that were in use, not least by the Tyrrhenian pirates that haunted those waters.[5]

Suggested crew: 20 to 30 men.

Dimensions: length overall: 57 feet (17.4m); beam: 9 feet 6 inches (2.9m); draft: 21 inches (533mm); freeboard: 2 feet (610mm).

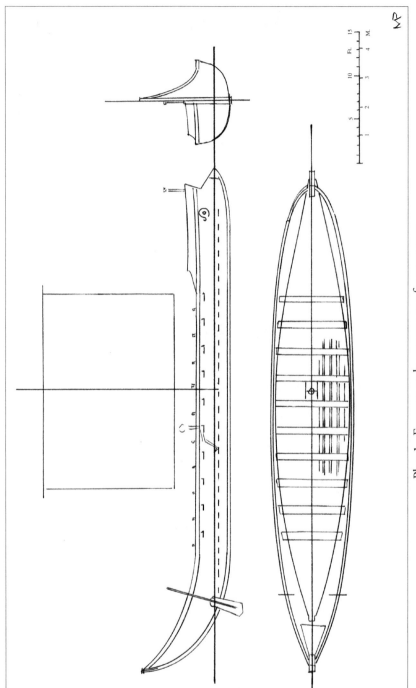

Plan 1. Etruscan-style monoreme of twenty oars.

Etruscan-style monoreme warship of thirty oars (Plan 2)

The vase or mixing bowl on which this is based (see Fig. 7) was found in south Italy, and the consensus of opinion holds that the ship on the left is Greek, being of a form commonly seen on Greek pottery, whereas that on the right (and shown here) is unlike any other depicted elsewhere (except on other Etruscan pottery) and generally held to be Etruscan. This is a not unreasonable assumption, given the provenance of the item and uniqueness of the design, so unlike anything Greek. It is, however, also commonly held to represent a merchant ship under attack, but I feel that it is actually a warship, as apart from the different bow form it is largely the same as the opposing Greek ship, only with the mast stepped whereas the Greeks have lowered theirs.

They are both monoreme conters, with their rowing quarters covered by a full-length deck, with open sides, supported by stanchions and from which the marines are fighting. The Etruscan ship has a different (but not impossible) bow as previously shown and must also have a crow's nest or mast platform, as a marine is shown on it, throwing a javelin.[6]

In considering the tactical reasons for such a bow form, it is suggested that it was intended for a different form of attack. Whereas the conventional ram was intended to hole an enemy at the waterline, the point of impact could, according to the motion of the antagonists, be anywhere between the underside of a hull and the level of the topmost oars.[7] With this ship a less critical aiming point was sought, and the intention seems to have been to override the enemy ram and cut into the upperworks of an opponent, rupturing bulwarks and decks and causing injury directly to the rowers and deck crews. How successful this concept may have been, if indeed such an interpretation is correct, is not known, but the Etruscans, having dominated the Tyrrhenian Sea for centuries and having bettered the Greeks off Alalia in 535 BC, had their seapower effectively ended when the Greeks severely defeated them off Cumae in 474 BC. In any event, the form does not appear to have been emulated by anyone else in the Mediterranean.

Although this illustration is considerably older (*c.* 650 BC) than the earliest known Roman warship, it is little more than a century after the end of Etruscan rule at Rome and nearly two centuries before Rome's acquisition of Naples with its Greek influence, and thus it is felt not unreasonable, as with the last ship, to presume that the earliest of Roman warships were based on Etruscan practice.

Suggested crew: 40 to 45 men.

Dimensions: length overall: 68 feet (20.7m); beam: 10 feet 6 inches (3.2m); draft: 3 feet (915mm).

Greek-style monoreme warship of fifty oars (penteconter) Colour Plate III (Plan 3)

Although earlier than the early fourth century BC, examples of this type can be found on an Athenian bowl of *c.* 600–550 BC,[8] showing twenty-two oars on the beam (a penteconter) and an Attic jug of *c.* 520 BC,[9] showing a similar ship with sixteen oars a side (a triaconter) (see Fig. 9). In both the heads of the rowers are indicated, rowing through ports in the upper bulwark. Horizontal lines are drawn above the bulwark and

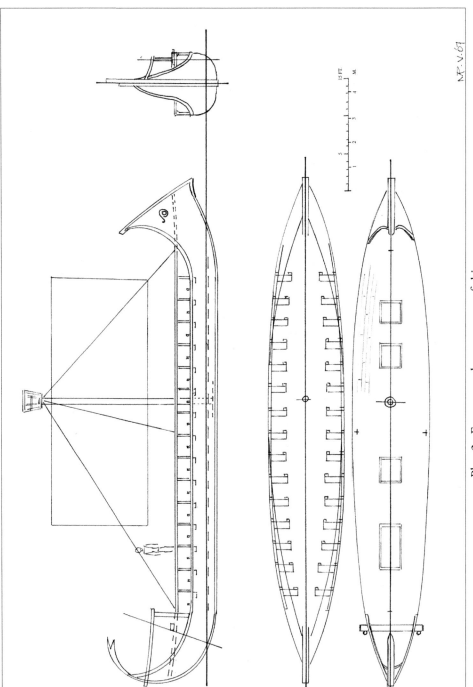

Plan 2. Etruscan-style monoreme of thirty oars.

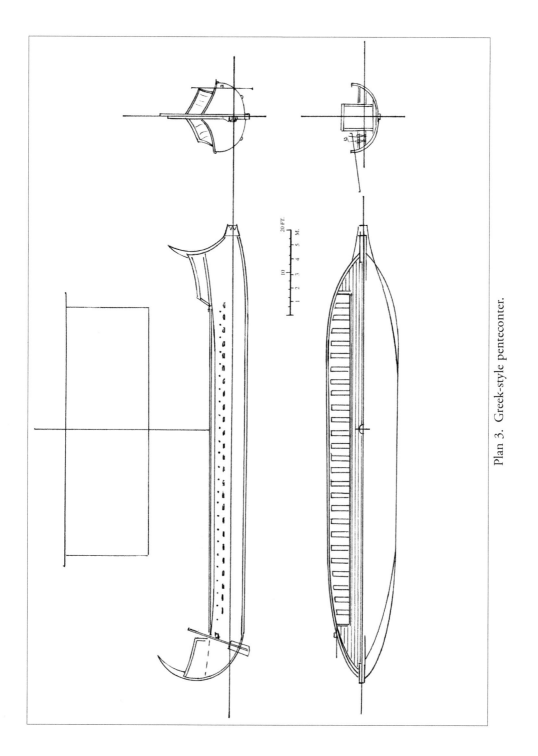

Plan 3. Greek-style penteconter.

Figure 42. Image of a ship with no decking covering at all above the rowers; Athenian, sixth century BC.

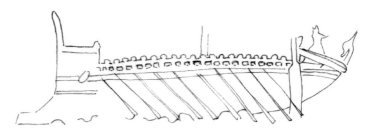

Figure 43. Monoreme conter showing a line bisecting the heads of the rowers, suggesting the presence of a flying deck, linking the bow and stern sections. Detail of an Athenian cup, *c.* 500 BC, British Museum.

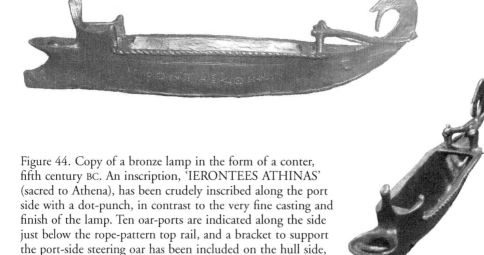

Figure 44. Copy of a bronze lamp in the form of a conter, fifth century BC. An inscription, 'IERONTEES ATHINAS' (sacred to Athena), has been crudely inscribed along the port side with a dot-punch, in contrast to the very fine casting and finish of the lamp. Ten oar-ports are indicated along the side just below the rope-pattern top rail, and a bracket to support the port-side steering oar has been included on the hull side, below the after deck. It is decked at bow and stern, with an open centre section.

slightly higher than the rowers' heads. The helmsman is shown sitting high in the stern looking over the rowers' heads and from which can be inferred a raised or decked-over stern deck for him. In the bow there is another raised deck with a bulwark or screen around it, highly decorated and obviously intended to act as a fighting platform for the embarked marines. Both ships are armed with a ram in the shape of an animal head and both carry a single mast amidships with a yard, square sail and buntlines or brails brought down to the deck.

The problem remaining to be interpreted is the midships section. Had just the heads of the rowers been shown as in the next example (Fig. 42), they could only be completely open boats with no decking other than at bow and stern (as in Fig. 44). It is the horizontal line above the heads that clouds the picture and both ships show it. It could represent one of two things, either a deck or perhaps a framework for mounting protective leather or wooden screens along the sides in action, or to raise the sides when in rough weather. In the left-hand (Greek) ship in Figure 7, a hull-length top deck is clearly shown, whereas in the triaconter, the helmsman seems to be sitting below the level of the topmost lines, which are still above the heads of the rowers. This appears to indicate a side framework. In the monoreme penteconter, the lines appear to in fact bisect the heads of the rowers and have thus been interpreted as a flying deck amidships to permit access fore and aft, space for the sailors to handle the rig and for stowage below.

A similar example is in Figure 43, which also shows a monoreme conter, rowed across the bulwark, although curiously, whereas ten oars are shown, twenty rowers' heads are included, perhaps to indicate that there were ten per side. In any event, a strong line spanning the poop and fore decks bisects the rowers' heads once again. Interestingly, a prominent and overscale stern rail is included, similar to that seen on the model in Figure 44.

There survives a bronze lamp, found on the Acropolis at Athens and dated to the end of the fifth century BC. The model of it in Figure 44 has a small stern deck with a prominent handrail either side, supported by stanchions. It is rendered substantially oversized for the scale, perhaps the result of the medium in which it is cast. There is also a small foredeck, bounded by a bulwark on either side of the stempost. The ram has been elongated to accommodate the dish for the wick of the lamp. The model scales to a length-to-beam ratio of 4.27 to 1,[10] more akin to the proportions of a merchantman, probably to the result of being modelled as a lamp, rather than a scale model.

As to rig, the portrayals of these ships on pottery show fairly shallow sails, bent to long yards. This may, of course, be a form dictated by the rather narrow horizontal bands forced upon the artists by the medium in which they worked, but the uniformity of the portrayals leaves one reasonably secure in assuming that this was the pattern of sails in reality. None of the ships has more than one mast.

Suggested crew: 60 to 65 men.

Dimensions: length overall 107 feet (32.6m); waterline: 103 feet (31.4m); beam overall: 16 feet (4.8m); waterline: 14 feet (4.3m); draft: 4 feet (1.22m); freeboard: 2 feet (610mm); length-to-beam ratio: 6.7 to 1.

BIREMES

Etruscan-style bireme warship (Plan 4)

Although the sources are earlier than ideal, there is no reason to suppose that similar types did not remain in service much later, and one of them (Fig. 45) shows an Etruscan ship at the end of the time of Etruscan dominance over Rome itself.

The bireme has a prominent, raised fighting platform in the bows, with screening extending well back along the hull and a stern deck for helmsman in the same fashion as the monoremes. The illustration also shows the bireme oar system, the lower reme worked through ports in the side and the upper by tholes set into the top wale, the oars of each reme being staggered in relation to the other. There are indications of structures amidships including a line of stanchions, but basically the same problem of whether the ship had decking above the rowers remains. In this example, figures are shown running forward along the level of what must be a deck (one such is included in the sketch amidships (in outline) to demonstrate this). In the stern is a decked area for the helmsmen (most of whom, with the sternpost, have been lost through damage). Amidships, the topmost reme of oars are shown against thole-pins which emerge from the top of the bulwark; although the oars are shown in place, they are unmanned. The omission of the rower's heads limits interpretation. Above this and detached from it is the deck linking the foredeck and poop deck, having downward projections which do not meet the bulwark as one might expect if it were an overall deck supported by stanchions thereon. From this it is posited that the downward projections indicate stanchions inboard of the rowers and thus a flying deck in the manner of the monoreme penteconter previously described. The step down from the poop deck and the lack of height between the bulwark and flying deck would also seem to confirm this. The interpretation allows for a deck 5 feet (1.52m) in width and similar headroom below it.

The forward section of the ship is different again, for whereas the bulwark line is continued, as evidenced by a line of ports extending forward, what would otherwise (and as shown in the Greek example below) be the foredeck side screens, appear in fact to be a raised platform, archers being shown on top of it (again, one is included in outline). The ship would therefore seem to have, if not quite a two-level forward section, at least a raised section forward. The problem when drawing the ship is that the placing of the archers totally above the foredeck structure (in what would be a completely exposed position) appears illogical. It only seems to make sense if the lower solid line, that is the one immediately above the ports, is the raised foredeck itself, which is also then the same level as the poop deck. This then leaves the structure above it as the foredeck bulwarks with the archers erroneously placed on top instead of within them. The figures on the flying deck are correctly placed, there being corroboration for placing them where they are (see, for example, Fig. 7). The vertical decorations on the bulwark would also support such an interpretation.

As to the rowing system, although only nine oars are discernable, there were obviously more, and twenty tholes can be seen along the bulwark. The trireme (with 170

Figure 45. Bireme warship. Detail from an Etruscan jug, *c.* 500 BC, British Museum, after Meijer.

oars) was being perfected at the same time as the pot from which this figure comes, and so it would be reasonable for this ship to have a greater number of oars than the pente-conter, perhaps as many as forty per side. Of the twenty tholes seen, however, only one in four has an oar attached, the scale of which would also preclude the addition of one per 'thole'. There would be little point, however, in contriving this much more compli-cated ship for the same power as before, so the number of oars in the reconstruction has arbitrarily, but not, it is suggested, unreasonably, been increased to sixty. Because of the bireme arrangement, this can be compressed into a shorter hull, only 87 feet (26.5m) as opposed to the 107 feet (32.6m) overall of the monoreme penteconter. With an overall beam of 15 feet (4.6m), the length-to-beam ratio of the hull is reduced from the tender 6.7 to 1 of the monoreme to a more handy and manoeuvrable 5.8 to 1, yet still having more motive power. There is no deck sheer in the central, rowing section of the hull, this being limited to the fore and poop decks. An animal-head ram has been added (the ram is missing on the original) in the manner of the Greek ships (see below) and the form of foredeck would allow a largish fore cabin below. No method can be seen for the securing of the steering oars and so simple catheads have been indicated on the drawing; this method can be attested by comparison with the 'Kyrenia wreck' of *c.* 300 BC and the working reproduction of it[11] and also of the cast example on the model ship in Figure 44. No rig is shown, but presumably, as with all the other ships, this would also be capable of mounting a mast, yard and sail.

Some reservations arose as the drawing progressed, particularly as to the difference between it and the original, in the forecastle, especially the relative size of the apertures below the foredeck. However, the original painting is constrained by the size, curve and height of the panel on the jug. Thus the ship becomes foreshortened and the need to indicate the usual overscale figures affects the vertical scale. Although this may appear as

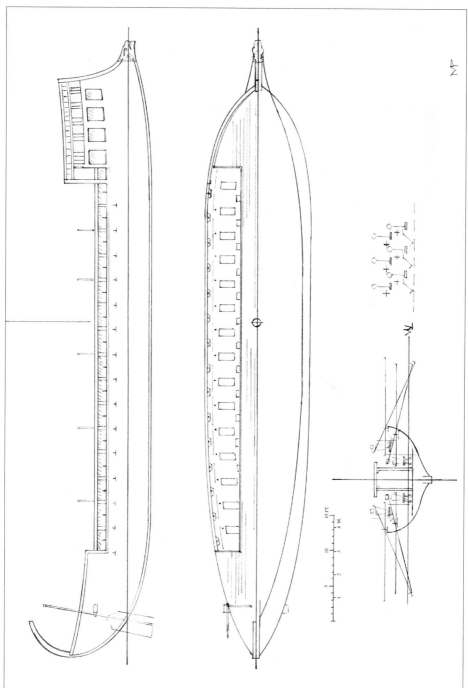

Plan 4. Etruscan-style bireme.

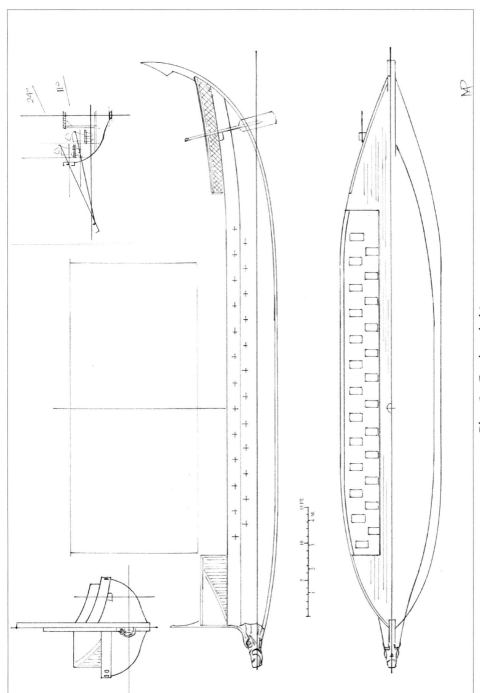

Plan 5. Greek-style bireme.

an excuse for the drawing (Plan 4), the variations between it and the original are mostly the result of the difference between an impressionist painting, subject to the constraints mentioned, and a scale drawing.

Suggested crew: *c.* 70 men.

Dimensions: length overall: 87 feet (26.5m); waterline : 81 feet 6 inches (24.8m); beam overall : 15 feet (4.6m); waterline : 13 feet (3.9m); draft: 3 feet 4 inches (1m); freeboard: 18 inches (455mm).

Oars: 60 at 14 feet (4.3m), gearing 3.5, worked at 13 and 24 degrees.

Greek-style bireme warship (Plan 5)

The two examples of the Greek style of bireme (Figs. 46 and 47) show an overall uniformity of style, both having elegant, curving sternposts, an open waist section and a raised, screened foredeck, ahead of which is a prominent ram in the form of a stylised animal head, probably a boar.

In the first example (Fig. 46) a framework is shown running amidships above the rowers' heads, but here the sailors' feet are shown level with the rowers' shoulders or heads, from which it seems clear that a central, flying deck runs the length of the ship, linking the bow and stern platform decks. The question here is the interpretation of the frame; it is either a handrail for the sailors on the flying deck or a frame for mounting protective screening along the top of the bulwarks. As two levels of rails are clearly shown, perhaps this ship had both.

The ship is depicted twice on the same cup, in the first instance (Fig. 46) under oar and sail, with twenty oars visible along the side. The upper oars are being worked across the bulwark and the lower oars, through oar-ports in the hull. In the second picture (Fig. 47), four of the crew can be seen trimming the sail. In this view, only eighteen of the oars can be counted along the side, from which it can be deduced that four of the oarsmen have shipped their oars and are the crew members now visible on deck. In neither view are any marines or other deck crew shown, apart from the helmsmen seated in the sternsheets, perhaps hanging on to the landing ladder which they appear to be losing over the stern.

In the second example (Fig. 48) the upper oars are rowed through oar-ports in the top wale, the lower through oarports in the hull as before; sixteen oars can be seen. The helmsmen sit in the stern, and although a small piece of horizontal rail can be seen immediately aft of the foredeck screening, it does not reappear at the stern (amidships is dominated on the original by a hugely overscale figure of a deity) and accordingly it would appear not to have a raised connecting or flying deck linking the two. The foredeck and poop deck levels are in line with the top of the top wale and unlike the last example, the poop has a low screening around it.

The foredecks of both are shorter than the Etruscan example and the ram is bigger. The only deck sheer is at the very stern. As with the Greek monoreme, the rig has a very long yard but a shallow sail, and the ship has fifty oars.

Suggested crew: 60 men.

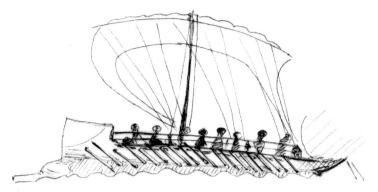

Figure 46. Greek bireme with central deck before some of the crewmen shipped and left their oars to attend to the rig. From an Athenian cup found at Vulci, showing two scenes of a warship and a merchant ship, *c.* 520 BC, British Museum.

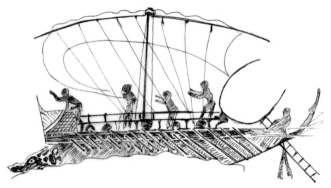

Figure 47. The same ship with some of the crew attending to the rig. Athenian, *c.* 520 BC.

Figure 48. Another Greek bireme, with no central deck and oar-ports for both remes; figures omitted for clarity. From a painted jug from Tarquinia, of Greek manufacture, *c.* 510 BC.

Dimensions: Length overall: 83 feet 6 inches (26.4m); waterline: 72 feet (22m); beam overall: 14 feet (4.3m); waterline: 12 feet (3.6m); draft: 3 feet (915mm); freeboard: 18 inches (1.06m).

Oars: 50 at 13 feet (3.96m); gearing 3.3, worked at 24 and 11 degrees.

TRIREMES

Colour Plate IV (Plan 6)

With their acquisition of Naples in 326 BC and expansion into Campania, the Romans actually gained Greek shipbuilding techniques and technology, as well as shipyards and their shipwrights and craftsmen, along with an extended coastline. It must be assumed that by then at least, therefore, they had added the trireme to their fleet. Although steadily extending their coastlines and possessions, the Romans do not seem to have needed ships larger than the trireme before the outbreak of the Punic Wars in 264 BC. That is not to say, however, that as a burgeoning power, eager to impress or overawe, prestige could have demanded that some be acquired.

Nevertheless, the Romans must have been aware of and even familiar with the form of ships larger than triremes, if only by observing developments in nearby Sicily and by their ally, Carthage. In 310 BC the Romans found it desirable and necessary to appoint a permanent 'Navy Board' or admiralty to oversee the building, provision and operating of ships of their navy.

The trireme had been developed in the eastern Mediterranean in the late sixth century BC, when a third reme of rowers was added, superimposed and outboard of the upper rowers of the bireme system. They plied their oars across an outrigger, which was fixed above the bulwark and outboard of the hull proper. This added a third or so more motive power to a ship which was only a little bigger, producing what by all accounts was the fastest of the ancient world's oared warships. The classic Athenian trireme was powered by no less than 170 oars, 62 thranites in the topmost reme, 54 zygites in the middle and another 54 thalamites in the lowest reme. The type was the principal warship making up the battlefleets of the Greek–Persian wars and the Peloponnesian Wars which followed (ending in 405 BC) and were built in their hundreds.

The trireme was definitely in service with the Romans at the outbreak of the First Punic War in 264 BC, twenty having been ordered and built to join those already in service at that time.[12] How like the Greek originals of nearly three centuries earlier these ships were it is impossible to say, but in Roman service the trireme was to endure and develop until its final appearance at the Battle of the Hellespont in AD 323.

For these earliest of Roman triremes and in the absence of any evidence to the contrary, one can only assume that they were not a lot different from their fifth-century BC predecessors (see the section on oar systems in Chapter 2 and Fig. 15) and it is upon this premise that the drawing is based.[13]

A variation may be represented by the terracotta model of a ship from Cyprus, of the fourth century BC (Fig. 49). It is clearly not a true scale model, and the accuracy of

Figure 49. Copy of a terracotta model of a trireme from Cyprus, fourth century BC.

Figure 50. The *Olympias*, a full-size reconstruction of a fifth-century BC Athenian trireme, built in 1987 and extensively tested at sea. She is now kept at the Averof Museum at Nea Faliro, near Athens.

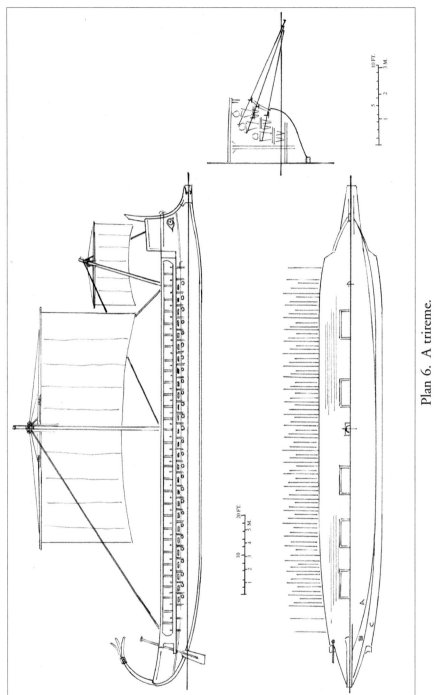

Plan 6. A trireme.

the rendition is again affected by the medium in which it is worked. It is from a time when the trireme as the mainstay of the battlefleets had passed, in favour of larger types. It may of course, have represented a bireme warship with a decorative, crenellated bulwark, but as the crenellations do not extend to the stem or where the raised bulwark crosses the stern and from the positioning of the indentations, this seems unlikely. If one assumes that the aft-most holes at zygite level are for the attachment of separate steering oars, a ship with nine each of thranite and zygite and seven of thalamite oar ports emerges, but in positions which seem reasonably balanced, even though far less so than in reality. The thranite oars are rowed across the indented bulwark, and the prominent ridge immediately below it and discernable on the inside of the hull on the other side could represent an outrigger, rendered less prominently than in reality. The prominent, squared-off forward ends of the outrigger/oar-box normally seen are here absent and the top wale is faired into the forepeak structure. This is possible in reality and could represent a later step in trireme evolution, along with the lack of any apparent covering deck.[14]

For the drawing, the Athenian model as established by the *Olympias* (Fig. 50) has largely been followed, and the rowing establishment, of sixty-two thranite, fifty-four zygite and fifty-four thalamite oars, retained. Other crew comprised four officers, six leading seamen, ten sailors, ten marines and four archers, a total of 204 men. The Romans can be guaranteed to have shipped a higher number of marines, as indeed did the Greek states other than Athens.

Dimensions: Length overall: 124 feet (37.8m); waterline: 116 feet (35.3m); beam overall: 16 feet (4.9m); waterline: 12 feet 6 inches (3.8m); draft: 3 feet 6 inches (1.07m); freeboard: 18 inches (457mm).

Oars: 14 feet (4.3m), gearing of 4, worked at 24, 19 and 11 degrees.

See colour plate IV.

NOTES

1 Livy, V.28.
2 Livy, I.56.
3 Polybius, III.22.
4 Polybius, III.22; III.25; III.27.
5 Ormerod, *Piracy in the Ancient World*.
6 This is a feature that does not appear on Greek ships. It is, however, shown on the ships of the antagonists in the reliefs at Medinet Habu of Rameses III's naval victory in 1176 BC.
7 Polybius, XVI.3.
8 Detail of an Athenian bowl; after Casson, original in the Louvre, Paris.
9 Detail of an Attic jug; after Casson, original in the Metropolitan Museum of Art, New York.
10 See also Johnston, *Ship and Boat Models in Ancient Greece*.
11 Bass, *A History of Seafaring*.

12 Polybius, I.20.

13 For detailed accounts of the design, building and operation of the *Olympias,* the full-size reconstruction of a trireme, see Morrison, Coates and Rankov, *The Athenian Trireme* and Welsh, *Building the Trireme.*

14 Conversely, the model could represent the 'Phoenician' type of trireme, without outrigger, as propounded by Morrison. Morrison and Coates, *Greek and Roman Oared Warships* and see Chapter 2, note 29, above.

5

NAVAL ASCENDANCY: THIRD AND SECOND CENTURIES BC

For Rome, the third century BC was dominated by the two great wars against Carthage (264–241 and 218–202 BC). The First Punic War was a struggle for possession of Sicily between Rome, which until then had been primarily a land power, and Carthage, primarily a naval power with a huge fleet that had dominated the western Mediterranean. Rome had, of course, operated naval forces for a long time, but in a limited way attuned principally to coastal defence, and in order to be able to compete, her navy had to grow from a few dozen to the several hundreds of ships that would be needed to be able to challenge and overcome the Punic Navy. This it did, and the Romans were to beat their opponents in all but one of the many naval battles that decided the war, including the last.

In the Second Punic War, the still-powerful Carthaginian Navy failed to effectively challenge Roman naval power, leaving it, in effect, to dictate the course of that war, and after victory leaving Rome as the dominant, indeed only, naval power in the western Mediterranean. In the following century, the Romans became embroiled in Greek and Hellenistic affairs and were drawn inexorably into the Aegean and eastern Mediterranean. The veteran fleets of the Punic Wars extended Roman naval primacy into those areas as well by the end of the century.

It was a period of huge expansion which saw the introduction, in quantity, of new types of warship. The principal warship type with which these wars were fought at sea was the 'five' or quinquereme.[1] 'Fours' or quadriremes came into use, although probably only in small numbers with the Romans. Both of these types had been invented and developed in the early fourth century BC, in the course of the rivalry between Syracuse and Carthage for hegemony over Sicily. The types had spread, Athens having examples of both in service by 324 BC, and they appeared at Alexander's siege of Tyre in 332 BC.[2] The navies of the western Mediterranean seem to have avoided the vast multiremes so beloved of the Hellenistic east, and the largest type known to have been in Roman service was a 'six' or *sexteres* ('sexireme' seems somehow wrong!).

Triremes and conteres remained in service in supporting roles,[3] but with the start of the Illyrian Wars in 229 BC, operations in the Adriatic brought the Romans into contact with a large number of the local native craft, the *lembus*, which they also captured. These became *liburna* (liburnian) to the Romans. This type they went on to take into their service and adopt as a light warship, following which it underwent considerable development and was to remain in widespread use over the course of the ensuing centuries.

The dichotomy in design philosophies of the Etruscans and Greeks, as we have already seen, completely disappears with the advent of the Punic Wars. Ship configurations or types (the quinquereme, *sexteres*, etc.) were built and adopted, doubtless with influence from their originators, but detailed design, building and further development were now part of a more homogenous Roman tradition. Along with the deployment of huge fleets of the big ships went the installation on them and the use of artillery and towers, as well as, of course, the *corvus* and its successor device.

THE 'SEXTERES'

Colour Plate V (Plan 7)
One of the very best renditions of what is unquestionably a Roman warship is the first-century BC relief found at Praeneste (Palestrina), north-east of Rome (Fig. 51), which shows a large, bireme warship with a tower mounted in the bows, diagonally to the ship's centre-line.[4] The stern section is missing; marines are shown in exaggerated size on deck behind a bulwark and apparently standing on top of the oarbox. There is a crocodile figurehead and a box above it with the head of perhaps a patron deity. Aft of this is a break in the bulwark for deploying the boarding bridge and aft of that again a bulwark with 'shield'-type decoration. Below this would appear to be a row of louvres for a ventilation course. An artemon or foremast is shown, without standing rigging or yard, but with a prominent bracket, doubtless of metal, securing it to the stempost. The ship could be any type between a quadrireme, the smallest type known to have mounted a tower, and a six or *sexteres*, the largest type known to have been in Roman service. The rendition of the ship gives an impression of massiveness, and it seems not unreasonable therefore to regard it as a *sexteres*. This type first came into use with the Romans during the First Punic War, two being flagships of the Roman fleet at the Battle of Ecnomus in 256 BC.[5] One appears in the fleet of Sextus Pompeius in Sicily in 36 BC,[6] and they were with Octavius' fleet at Actium in 31 BC. The grave stela of a crewman from a *sexteres* at Misenum confirms that there was at least one in service in the early imperial period. By this time, however, with no warships other than Roman ships, it had no enemies, had become a dinosaur and was probably retained for prestige, perhaps as a memorial, or just to keep the technology of building and operating such a ship alive. These reasons became less important and disappeared, with the last of these ships, by the mid- to late first century AD.

There has been discussion as to the oar system shown by the relief, in that two levels of oars are clearly and deliberately shown emerging, the topmost from outboard of the lower and through a kind of articulated socket; alternatively, this may represent the *askomata*, fitted to prevent the ingress of water.[7] Above them there is what could be construed as a third reme with the oars shipped and pulled inboard, so that only the very

Figure 51. Relief of a large Roman warship from Praeneste (Palestrina), north-east of Rome. First century BC. Vanni/Art Resource, NY.

Figure 52. The Praeneste relief as a trireme.

Figure 53. The relief as a bireme.

ends of them remain visible. Apart from there being too many 'oar ends' of the wrong shape, such an arrangement would not allow, on what is otherwise an accurate representation of the ship, for any ventilation course (see Chapter 3). It would, however, explain the discrepancy in the relative height of the marines. On the two marines outboard of it, the bulwark comes up to mid-thigh, whereas on those inboard of it, where the figures are the same size, it rises only to mid-shin, the difference in deck heights being the space occupied by the thranite reme (Fig. 52). The geometry is difficult, however, and it is probably more reasonable to hold that a bireme is what is intended and shown, the arrangement above being a side deck, jettied out on a line of brackets to allow a ventilation course and protected in this way from plunging missiles (Fig. 53).

So, given that it is a very large bireme, it is always possible that the relief shows a quadrireme, with two men per oar, but the sculpture seems altogether more massive and has therefore been interpreted and modelled as a six. Further reflection on oar systems prompts the question why such an arrangement, although workable, would have been chosen. As a bireme (Fig. 53), each oar crew of three men applies respectively 1, 0.8 and 0.6 'manpower' to each oar; multiplied by two, gives 4.8 manpower per group of two oars. In a trireme arrangement (Fig. 52), however, two men per oar apply 1.8 manpower per oar; multiplied by three, yields 5.4 manpower per group of six rowers, over half a manpower more from the same crew for little extra complication in the internal arrangement of the ship. Thus more propulsive power at more or less the same cost (the 'six' as a trireme, Fig. 54). The gearing of the oar also changes for each rower, relative to his position, thus for the inboard man in the plan the gearing is 3.3, for the next man outboard of him it rises to 4.2 and for the outermost man is as high as 6. Against this, however, in compensation, they respectively apply these gearings through progressively smaller spans. Whereas the bireme six arrangement seems eminently reasonable, it is difficult to imagine any reason why the ever-practical Romans would prefer this when they must have known the relatively greater power of the 'engine room' in a trireme arrangement. However, in such an evidently large ship, perhaps the height of a thranite reme would result in their having to work their oars at a larger angle from the horizontal (see Chapter 2), making them more difficult and less efficient to use. It has been found in practice that thranite oars at 30 degrees or more from the horizontal are 'uncomfortable' to work and far less efficient.[8] While considering the angle at which an oar is worked, allowance must be made for rougher water and the roll of a ship, both of which would affect the angle at which the oar enters, passes through and leaves the water on each stroke.

As a bireme, the rowers operate their oars at more modest angles (22 and 11 degrees), and there is a more roomy, simpler internal arrangement. Only the inboard rowers of each oar need to be trained, as they set the stroke and the other men simply add muscle. The ships were designed as floating fortresses, with their weight of artillery and overwhelming numbers of marines, rather than as self-propelled missiles, like the triremes. With them, ramming was a matter of opportunity rather than a deliberate practice, and whereas these big ships could not hope to compete with the lighter types when it came

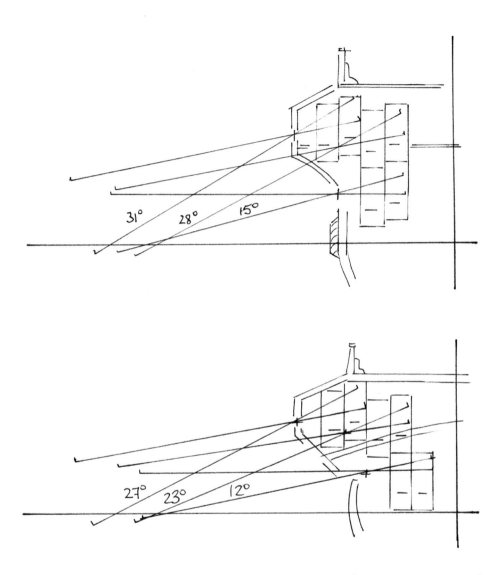

Figure 54. The *sexteres* as a trireme, alternative cross-sections. In the upper arrangement, the beam overall is 28 feet (8.53m), waterline 22 feet (6.7m). The deck is 13 feet 9 inches above water (4.2m). In the lower arrangement, the beam overall is also 28 feet (8.53m) and waterline of 20 feet (6.1m). The deck is 12 feet 6 inches (3.8m) above waterline and the freeboard for both ships is 3 feet (914mm). Both utilise a 26-foot (7.9m) oar with a gearing of 3.3. In both, the angle at which the oars are operated is higher than desirable, and the fore and aft spacing for the rowers would need careful attention in design to give sufficient clearance between them.

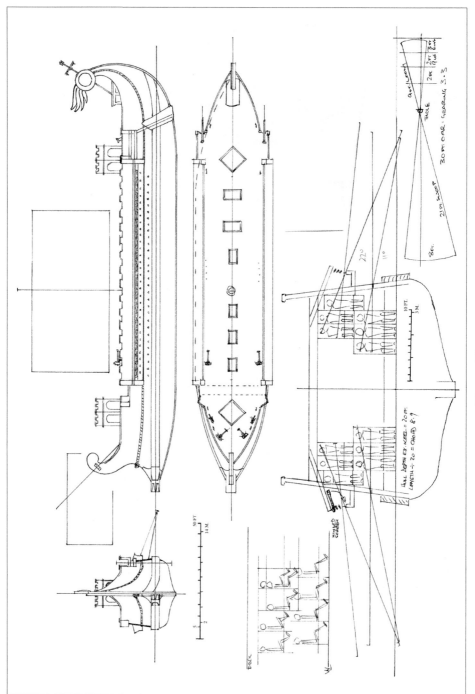

Plan 7. The *sexteres*.

to speed, their sheer mass would ensure that a collision, even at the very lowest closing speeds, would be highly injurious to a lighter vessel.

Suggested crew: 15 officers, 30 sailors, 80 marines, 30 archers, 24 artillerymen, 180 thranite rowers, 180 zygite rowers; total: 539.

Dimensions: length overall: 186 feet (56.7m); waterline: 178 feet (54.2m); beam overall: 34 feet (10.4m); waterline: 32 feet (9.75m); draft: 8 feet 6 inches (2.6m); freeboard: 3 feet (915mm).

Oars: 120 at 30 feet (9.14m), gearing 3.3.

THE QUINQUEREME

Colour Plate VI (Plans 8 and 9)

The quinquereme, which formed the backbone and bulk of the first-rate combat ships of the antagonists in the Punic Wars, evolved from prototypes built for Dionysius, the Tyrant of Syracuse, the first emerging in about 398 BC.[9] Having been adopted by the Carthaginians as the mainstay of their battle formations, in order to oppose them, the Romans had to build their own. It is an old saw, but for various reasons, the first Roman quinqueremes were not copied from a stranded Punic one,[10] being totally different, bulkier, heavier and designed to be operated differently. Tactically, the big difference was, of course, the introduction and use of the *corvus*, supported by the mounting of towers by the Romans, all designed to bypass the acknowledged Carthaginian superiority in experience and seamanship and to enable their superior infantry to board the enemy, supported by covering fire. Such installations proved to be decisive in battle but unfortunately adversely affected the ship's stability and seakeeping abilities, and literally hundreds of these early types were lost to storms.[11]

Later in the Punic War, the Romans did actually capture a Punic 'five'; it was in fact the ship of a notorious Rhodian blockade runner and renowned for its speed.[12] It was the lessons learned from this ship, and their own bitter experience, that the Romans embodied in their later quinqueremes, which led to a lighter, faster and altogether more handy and more seaworthy ship and with which they successfully concluded the war. By the outbreak of the Second Punic War in 218 BC, there were no fewer than 220 in service.[13]

More than any other type, the quinquereme was the weapon with which the Roman Navy became the dominant and ultimately the only Mediterranean naval power. It remained in widespread front-line service until the founding of the Imperial Navy in the twenties BC. Thereafter, and like the *sexteres* and with no naval rivals, they became unnecessary, and only a few remained in service, probably entirely disappearing as a type by the late first century AD, after over three centuries of use.

Apart from use in the battle formations of the Roman Navy, the quinquereme became a 'maid-of-all-work'. It was used in sieges, for the marine assault on Syracuse in 214 BC,[14] in Greece in 210 BC after first landing siege artillery,[15] and at Utica in 203 BC. Quinqueremes acted as troop transports, carrying and landing a legion[16] and thirty more

Figure 55. Reproduction of a Republican bronze denarius of the Second Punic War period showing the prow of what is possibly a quinquereme (author's collection).

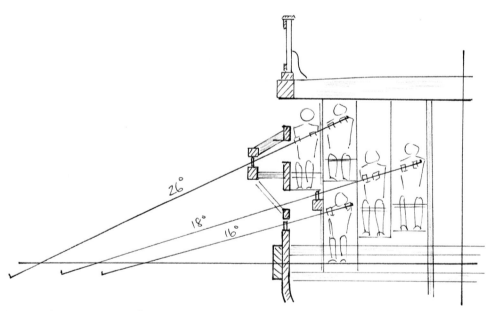

Figure 56. Cross-section of a quinquereme showing the rowing system.

escorted Scipio from Ostia to Empurias in Spain.[17] Diplomatic missions were added to their duties when five ships were sent with a delegation to King Attalus of Pergamum 'in a manner worthy of the dignity of Rome'[18] and three more were sent to King Philip of Macedon.[19] More in keeping with their designed function, however, was their frequent use for raiding enemy coasts and harbours.[20]

Despite many hundreds having been built, no representation survives that can be unequivocally categorised as a quinquereme. Many of the coins issued by the Romans during these centuries featured the prow of a warship (Figs. 6 and 40), all of which were very similar in rendition. It is not unreasonable to assume that the quinquereme, the principal type in service, was the type that was represented on the coins (Fig. 55). Once again, the problem in interpretation is the variety of things about the bows. As any attempt at interpretation without corroboration must be purely conjectural, a more conventional approach to the form of the foredeck has been adopted here (Plans 8 and 9) and the superscribed details on the coins translated as impressionist indications of the *corvus*, artillery or even of victory figures symbolically floating above the prows (see the coin of Antonius, Fig. 6).

A few further details emerge from the literature. For example, the number of rowers in each Roman quinquereme at the Battle of Ecnomus in 256 BC was 300.[21] This has been interpreted as representing three remes of thirty oars per side, 180 oars in total.[22] As to handling, in a battle in the Straits of Gibraltar against some Punic ships in 206 BC, 'the Roman quinquereme, perhaps because her size steadied her, or because her more numerous oars made her easier to control in the tide-rip, sank two triremes and sheared off the oars from the side of a third'.[23]

As to dimensions, the upper deck height was *c.* 10 feet (3m) above water, slightly less as it was related in Roman feet (11⅝ inches/296mm) or 9 feet 3 inches (2.96m).[24] The deck height was mostly dictated by the need to accommodate the rowers below and thus also by the number of remes. It is also desirable to limit the height above water because most of the weight was above the waterline, perhaps as much as three-quarters of it. The crew alone would weigh in the region of 23 tons, all above the waterline. Conversely, a higher deck would confer an advantage in a fight against ships with lower deck heights. As to length, allowing a reme of thirty oars (ante) at an interscalmium of 3 feet (915mm), with space at each end, gives an 'engine room' length of 96 feet (29.2 m); add, say, 30 feet (10m) for the bow section and another 35 feet (10.6m) for the stern and an overall length of about 160 feet (48.76m) results.

All of the preceding remarks apply to the form that the oar system took. The most likely system, however, is a trireme arrangement with two rowers at each oar in the upper two remes and a single rower at the thalamite level. This brings us back however, to the principle maintained earlier, that all the oars had to be more or less of the same length. It does not seem possible, given the geometry of the 'five', to achieve this, not least as the thalamite oarsman would be trying single-handedly to work a two-man oar. Of course, it is always possible that the 'five' was rowed as a bireme with three thranites above two zygites per oar, rather in the manner of the *sexteres* (see above).[25] If this were

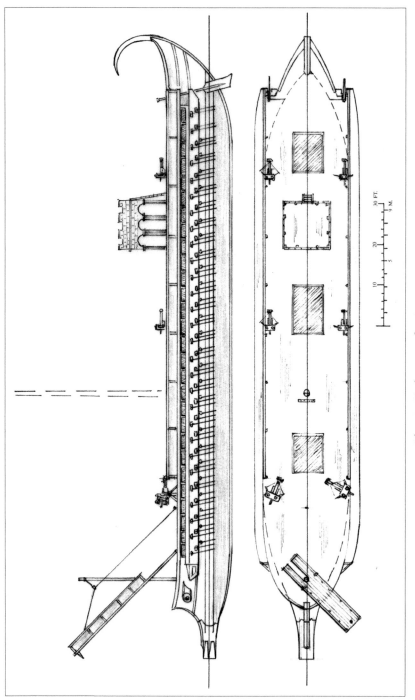

Plan 8. Early type of quinquireme.

30 FT.
10   20
5   9 M.

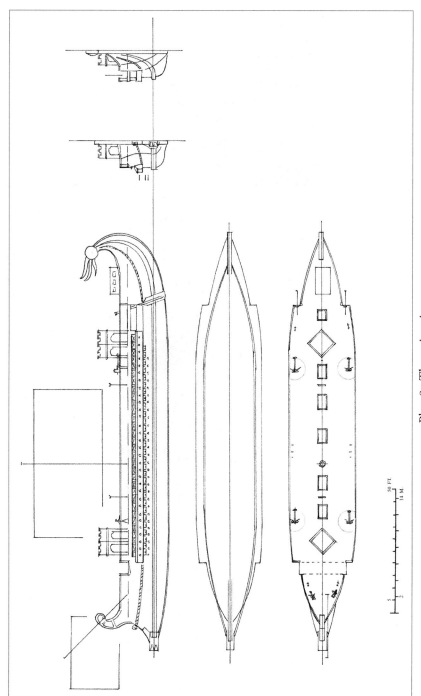

Plan 9. The quinquireme.

so, it would suggest that it preceded, and by the addition of one more zygite rower, became the *sexteres*. That the latter did not supersede the quinquereme was presumably because the *sexteres* did not offer a big enough advantage. If this were so, then the relative sizes of the two types should be more similar than suggested here.

Assuming a trireme, however, and that the thalamite oars are shorter, then provided that the gearing of all of the oars is the same, it should be possible for the thalamite rowers to synchronise their oar-strokes with the others.[26] However, the shorter oar passes through a smaller arc than the upper two, and having less mass will move more quickly. The thalamite rower must either slow to match his oar-stroke to the others or maintain a faster striking rate, perhaps with a higher-geared oar, which was possible as he was operating clear from the other oars.[27] Experimentation with a working model of the system is needed to resolve the question.

In the reconstructions, two types of Roman quinquereme have been represented, the first (Plan 8) being their initial design of circa 264 BC and equipped with the *corvus*. The second (Plan 9) is intended to show the later, refined type, with the boarding bridge. Both are arranged as triremes (Fig. 56).

Suggested crew: 8 officers; 20 sailors; 40 marines (plus a century, 80 men, in the First Punic War); 124 thranite rowers (early type: 112); 116 zygite rowers (early type: 112); 56 thalamite rowers (early type: 104); total rowers: 296 (early type: 328); total crew: 364 (early type: 396).

Dimensions (early type): length overall: 154 feet (47m); waterline: 142 feet (43m); beam overall: 26 feet (8m); waterline: 20 feet (6m); draft: 4 feet 6 inches (1.37m); freeboard: 2 feet (610mm).

Dimensions (later type): length overall: 169 feet (51.5m); waterline: 158 feet (48m); beam overall: 26 feet (8m); waterline: 22 feet (6.7m); draft: 6 feet (1.8m); freeboard: 2 feet (610m).

THE QUADRIREME

Colour Plate VII (Plan 10)

The Carthaginians were credited by Pliny with the invention of the quadrireme. [28] The most likely method for rowing one of these was as a bireme with two men per oar. A type much beloved of the Rhodians and known to have been in Carthaginian service,[29] they were also built and employed in small numbers in Roman service, where captured examples were also pressed into use. The type, although not as high[30] and powerful as a quinquereme, was popular, efficient and probably economical to operate as well as being a good seaboat and big enough to mount a tower and some artillery. The type is recorded as in service with both of the Italian Imperial Fleets in the early second century AD, the names of eleven being known from grave stelae at Misenum and a further six from stelae at Ravenna. As a type, they are not attested beyond the early second century AD and probably disappeared in the third century crises.

There are several reasons to believe that the wall paintings at Herculaneum (Colour

Plate I) are likely to show quadriremes. Firstly, both paintings show squadrons of similar ships,[31] all of which have a single, massive tower with a rounded front, mounted slightly ahead of amidships, as opposed to the twin fore- and aft-mounted towers that one would expect and which could be carried by the larger quinqueremes and sixes. Secondly, in both paintings the artist has indicated that the ships have more than one reme by brush strokes at the forward end of the oars. On two of the ships, the artists has clearly shown two levels (Fig. 57B and C). While the impressionistic style of the paintings must be allowed for (see Chapters 1 and 2), it seems reasonable to conclude that a bireme is indicated. Thirdly, quadriremes were definitely in service at the base at Misenum, just across the Bay of Naples when these paintings were executed (early first century AD).

One other indication exists, the only one that is actually labelled as to type, namely the graffito at Alba Fucens (Chapter 2, Fig. 10). This is a little indistinct and unfinished but does show a bow form similar to the Herculaneum paintings and a lattice-work bulwark. Alternatively, this could represent a ventilation course and deck without bulwark. Only the barest outline is shown and no real conclusions can be drawn.

Other than the general appearance of the ships, some further details can be discerned from the paintings (Colour Plate I). All of the ships are of the same type with the same distinctive shape of stem, bow and stern; they seem to have outriggers and a ventilation course and a gap in the deck bulwark at the forward end of the oar-box for slinging a boarding bridge (see Chapter 3 and Fig. 57A, B and C). The figures on deck are not too exaggerated in size relative to the ship, and the men manning the towers are shown without the discs that signify shields and are therefore perhaps archers. The shields are circular in shape, unlike the ovoid legionary body shield in use at this period. Presumably the latter was found to be too cumbersome for shipboard use; it may simply be that the circular disc was easier to paint and detailed accuracy regarding the shape of shields was unnecessary. On some of the ships, a man is shown at the top of the stempost, a lookout perhaps. Further, it would seem that the men in the bow section are at a higher level that those in the waist of the ship, indicating a foredeck at a higher level than the main deck of the ship. Some other corroboration would be needed before such a conclusion could be drawn, rather than relying solely on these indistinct paintings.

There is no sign at all of a sailing rig. Not only that, but with the tower amidships and occupying the position where a mainmast would be stepped, unless some arrangement for masting fore and aft of the tower (a two-masted ship in fact, which is not attested) was mounted, then with the exception of an artemon, these ships would appear, unusually, to be without any rig at all, or the facility to erect one. There is also no sign of anything that might indicate the mounting of artillery, although this may be 'lost' in the indistinct mass lining the decks. Finally, it is not clear whether the towers were mounted square-on or diagonally to the centre-line of the ships. In Colour Plate I, a faint vertical line on the lower right-hand ship in the upper photograph and the lower left-hand ship in the lower photograph could be indicating the latter.

Figure 57 (extracts from Colour Plate I).

A Top photograph, top ship. General arrangement, overall view, noting prow type, gap for boarding bridge, single midships tower, 'blank' horizontal course between oars and (shield-hung) bulwark, prominent housing covering port-side steering oar.

B Detail showing two remes (see also C, below). Note stanchions of ventilation course below bulwark and shields.

C Top photograph, lower right-hand ship. Noting oculus or eye painted on bow, shape of stem, lookout atop stempost, indication of two remes, tower, clear horizontal course representing ventilation course between oars and bulwark, the latter of panels between stanchions and top rail.

D Detail showing projecting oar-boxes or outriggers on port sides, as also seen on lower left-hand ship in top photograph.

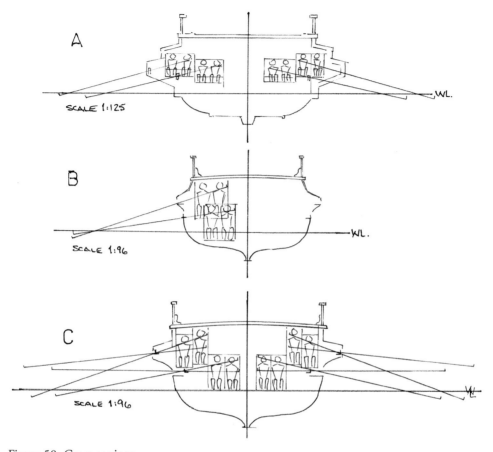

Figure 58. Cross-sections.

A The converted plastic kit. Twenty-five-foot (7.62m) oars; gearing 3; worked at 15 and 12 degrees.

B A quadrireme to fit the Piraeus ship-sheds. Beam 18 feet (5.5m) overall. Note: very crowded arrangement and the interscalmium must be carefully adjusted to allow space between the rowers and prevent the lower reme from fouling the upper. Twenty-one-foot (6.4m) oars; gearing 3; worked at 18.5 and 10 degrees.

C A better arrangement with an overall beam of 24 feet (7.3m) and waterline beam of 18 feet (5.5m); draft 4 feet 6 inches (1.37m); deck height 8 feet (2.6m) and freeboard of 2 feet (610mm). Oars are 24 feet (7.3m), gearing 3.04 and worked at 19 and 12 degrees. The drawing is of this version.

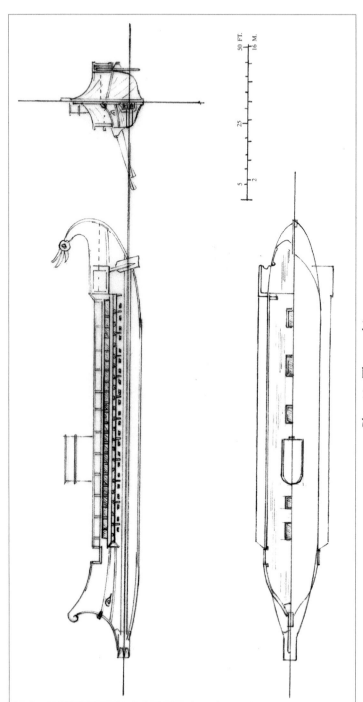

Plan 10. The quadrireme.

Records survive as to the crew muster of a Rhodian quadrireme and are given in the second column:[32]

officers	7	in the plastic model illustrated:	7
leading ratings	10		10
sailors	10		10
marines	20		30
archers	6		12
artillerymen	2		12
rowers, thranite	80		100
rowers, zygite	80		100
totals	215		281

The model (in Colour Plate VII) is from a much-modified plastic kit by Academy, interpreted as a quadrireme and adjusted to a scale of 1:125. This results in a ship of 135 feet (41m), a beam overall of 33 feet (10m) and 23 feet 6 inches (7.1m) at the waterline. The rowers are arranged in two remes of twenty-five oars on each side with two men to each oar of 23 feet (7m) and thus a little bigger than the Rhodian example. The deck height scales to 9 feet (2.7m) above the waterline, whereas about 7 feet (2.13m) would seem more likely and accord with the fact that marines from a quadrireme could not climb onto the higher deck of a quinquereme, which was at least 10 feet (3.1m) above water (see note 10). Although the ships were known to be beamy, the model is rather too broad (Fig. 59A). Quadriremes are recorded at Athens in the fourth century BC, and if they were housed in the ship sheds in the military harbour of Piraeus, the beam must have been limited to the width of those sheds, namely 19 feet 9 inches (6m) at the widest. Of course, they might not have been housed there, but such a beam is demonstrably practical (Fig. 58B).

Using the Rhodian crew muster of eighty thranite and eighty zygite rowers and the cross-section from Figure 58C, a reme of twenty oars emerges. The initial drawing based upon this produced a ship of 125 feet (38.1m) overall, which although obeying the parameters, seemed to lack the desired size and power. An overall length somewhere between that of a trireme (*c.* 125 feet) and a quinquereme (*c.* 165 feet) seemed appropriate. The problem is that as a combat ship, the quadrireme should be superior to a trireme, which it superseded in the battle line, yet inferior to a quinquereme, as we are told as much by the sources. The classic trireme had 170 oars and rowers and the quinquereme about 150 oars with about 300 rowers. One could thus expect the quadrireme to have perhaps as many as 120 oars, pulled by some 240 rowers, in remes of up to thirty. This would give the mid-way point and a ship the posited required size of about 145 feet in length.

The problem lies with the hard evidence of the Rhodian crew list, which limits the reme to twenty. Morrison in *Greek and Roman Oared Warships*, in making an interpretation of the Alba Fucens graffito (Fig. 10), finds that the ship had a reme of twenty-two oars, which would require 176 rowers and this has been adopted here to increase the ship under consideration.

The drawing (Plan 10) has thus been prepared on the basis of the Herculaneum ships with the various details noted (Fig. 57) and the dimensions adjusted as indicated above. This has yielded a ship of 145 feet overall, with a larger tower, which seems in keeping with the iconography, but at only eighty-eight oars, it still seems underpowered. The resulting vessel is quite compact, yet with a more generous beam, offering roomy accommodation for the rowing crew. The fact that it was lower than a quinquereme and beamier than a trireme also helps to account for the type's reputation for being a good seaboat (Fig. 58C), while maintaining the proportions in the paintings.

Dimensions: length overall: 145 feet (43.3m); waterline: 132 feet (40m); beam overall: 24 feet (7.3m); waterline: 18 feet (5.5m); draft: 4 feet 6 inches (1.37m); freeboard: 2 feet (610mm).

Oars: 4 remes of 22; 88 at 24 feet, gearing 3.04, worked at 12 and 19 degrees.

THE 'LIBURNA'

(Plans 11 and 12)

The form that the early examples of these boats took is a matter for considerable conjecture and attributable illustrations are non-existent. As originally built, they are described variously as 'as a lightly built, open galley without a ram, carrying about fifty men and rowed in a single reme';[33] 'of not more than sixteen oars' (presumably per side);[34] 'carrying twenty men and two horses in addition to the crew'.[35] The sources do seem in agreement that the ships were smallish with relatively large beam and without rams.[36] They had fine lines, particularly forward, for speed and were faster than other classes of light warship (saving probably triremes). There is no mention of any sailing rig. The Romans captured many of them,[37] and obviously found them useful, adopting them for scouting and communications duties, to the extent that they replaced the previously used types, such as penteconters. Perhaps before they took the type over, versions of it had evolved with a ram and some decking and protection for the rowers, some perhaps with the centre section of oars on each side manned by two men per oar (was this in fact the hemiolia of the Greeks?). There may even have existed bireme versions of it, but the Romans certainly developed a version of it as a bireme, with a ram.[38] The type evolved and grew into several variants at different times and in different theatres of operation, all retaining the generic name and remaining in widespread service for centuries, in forms which eventually had nothing in common with their Illyrian originals, save the name.

The difficulty when trying to picture these craft is in finding some form that fits the descriptions, or at least an average of them, but which is not related to contemporary Roman or Greek types. As an admittedly totally arbitrary starting point, I have taken the rather unusual and obviously local type of boat from the Illyrian coast, an example of which is displayed at the Maritime Museum in Split (Fig. 59). This example is approximately 36 feet (11m) long by 10 feet (3m) beam and stands about 4 feet (1.9m) high from the ground at the ends. As it stands, it is not possible to envisage it accommodating rowers, there being no evidence of a bulwark or other mountings for tholes,

Figure 59. Type of local craft of the Dalmatian coast. It has at some point been cut down to the present level to form a punt. Since being laid up, a temporary framework of battens has been inserted to retain the shape.

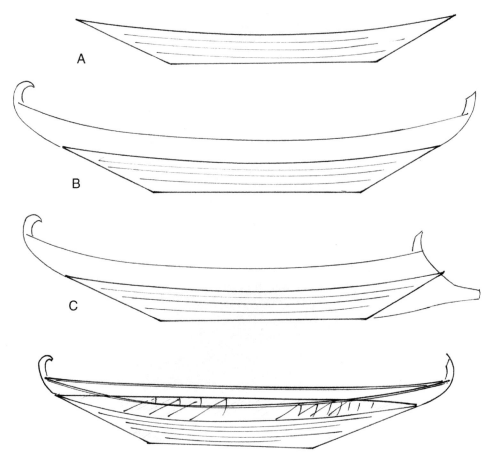

Figure 60. Genesis of the liburnian. The 'Split boat', elevation in approximate outline (A), with added bulwarks to produce a *lembus/liburna* (B) and with the addition of a ram, the *pristis* (C).

or thwarts, and the boat appears to have been cut down to form a sort of punt. The overall form does, however, bear comparison with surviving ancient merchant hulls, particularly the two larger examples in the Ship Museum at Ostia (although the Split boat is built frame-first).

Given these admittedly tenuous links and using the assumption that upperworks need to be added to give a workable vessel, the 'Split boat' with a reduced length-to-beam ratio of perhaps 5:1 can be developed to provide a *liburna* (Fig. 60A and B). This leads also to the *pristis*, in service from about 150 to 30 BC and described as a small warship with a ram, of *liburna* type.[39] Using the same basis to evolve a *pristis* (Fig. 60C) would complement the (ramless) *liburna*, at least as an interim and until the latter was developed to the stage where it acquired a ram and the types merged.

The drawing (Plan 11) therefore uses the basic shape of the 'Split boat', arranged to accommodate thirty rowers and therefore of the larger type, as a demonstration of how such an evolution could take place. Presumably the shell-first building method would give a hull strong enough to obviate the need for stiffening thwarts. Perhaps trusses were inserted to prevent the hull from splaying when hauled out of the water. In the lower drawing, the same shape has been used, with the addition of a ram and small raised internal decks in the bow to provide a small fighting platform and in the stern to improve the captain and helmsman's position, to form a *pristis*.

Dimensions for the *liburna*: length overall 76 feet 6 inches (23.3m); length waterline 56 feet (17m); beam overall 15 feet (4.57m); beam waterline 11 feet (3.35m); minimum freeboard 2 feet 3 inches (680mm); draft 18 inches (457mm); length/beam ratio 5.3:1 (waterline 5:1); chord 4 feet 9 inches (1.45m).

Thirty oars of 14 feet (4.26m) at 16 degrees; gearing (3 feet and 11 feet) = 3.6.

In the third drawing (Plan 12), the same basis has been enlarged to a bireme version with a doubling of the number of rowers and thus the motive power for only a slight increase in length, but an increase of a foot (300mm) in draft. With the increased height of the hull, stiffening thwarts have been introduced, and by deleting the forward two rowers on each side the forward fighting platform could be increased to a more practical size.

Dimensions for the bireme: length overall 80 feet (24.4m); beam overall 16 feet 6 inches (5.03m); freeboard 18 inches (457mm); draft 2 feet 6 inches (762mm).

Sixty oars of 16 feet (4.8m), gearing 3.5, worked at 16 degrees and 6 degrees.

THE 'CELOX'

Colour Plate VIII (Plan 13)

This was a small vessel, without a ram and built for speed. It was used for carrying despatches and other communications and for conveying senior officers about, a type of despatch and liaison craft. It was employed by most navies between the fifth and first centuries BC.[40]

A *celox* could be powered by anything between two and twelve oars, and with such a

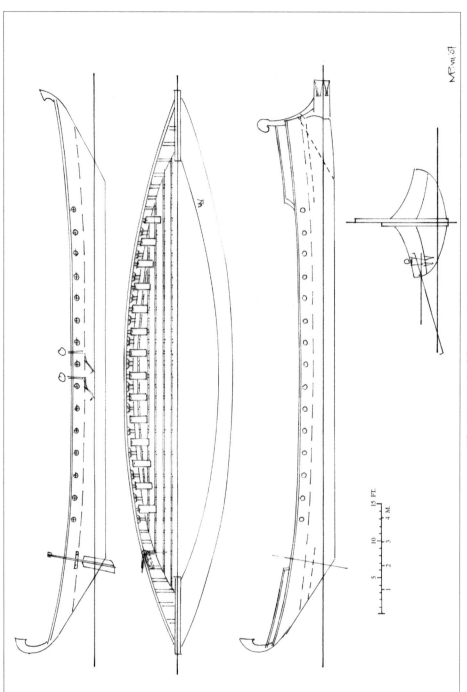

Plan 11. Early *liburna* and *pristis*.

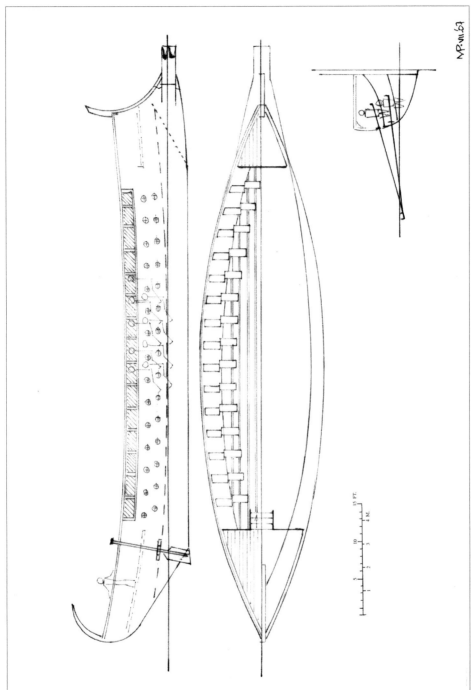

Plan 12. Early bireme *liburna.*

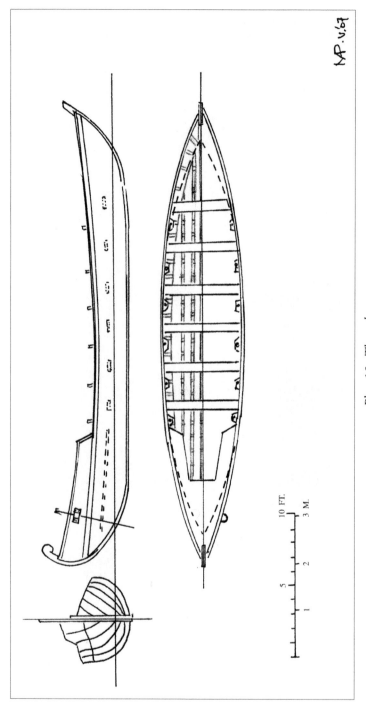

Plan 13. The *celox*.

wide variation it is clear that no single pattern of *celox* existed. It may well be that the designation referred not to a specific type of boat, but rather to any boat so used, that is, the term '*celox*' referred to the duty, not to the boat performing it. Whatever it was, it was a mono-reme, having been listed with other types as '*triereis, dikrota kai keletes*',[41] or 'three, two and *keletes* (celoces)', which are therefore, by extension, mono-remes. It was also a light vessel, having been described as '*naves longae centum sexaginta, celoces duodecim*',[42] namely 160 warships and twelve light vessels, or literally 'long ships 160, celoces 12'.

The reconstruction is purely conjectural and purports to show a twelve-oared *celox*, (for an eight-oared example, see Colour Plate VI, the photograph of the later quinquereme model).

NOTES

1 For example, Polybius at I.20.
2 Casson, *Ships and Seamanship.*
3 For example, Livy, XXI.17 and XXI.22; Polybius, I.20.
4 Now in the Vatican Museum.
5 *Sexteres* at Ecnomus: Polybius, I.26; Livy, XXIX; see also Caesar, *Civil War* II.1.5.
6 Appian, *The Civil Wars.*
7 For example, Morrison and Coates, *Greek and Roman Oared Warships.*
8 Welsh, *Building the Trireme.*
9 Diodorus Siculus, XIV.42, quoted in Torr, *Ancient Ships.*
10 Despite Polybius duplicating his own account at I.20 and I.59; and see below.
11 Pitassi, *The Navies of Rome.*
12 Polybius, I.59.
13 Livy, XXI.17.
14 Livy, XXIV.34.
15 Livy, XXVIII.5 and 6 and XX.10.
16 Livy, XXIV.36.
17 Livy, XXVI.19.
18 Livy, XXIX.11.
19 Livy, XXX.26.
20 For example, Livy, XXV.31.
21 Polybius, I.26.
22 Morrison and Coates, *Greek and Roman Oared Warships.*
23 Livy, XXVIII.30.
24 Morrison and Coates, *Greek and Roman Oared Warships*, quoting Orosius (fifth century AD), who could never have seen one but may well have had access to information or sources since lost to us.
25 And as posited by Casson, *Ships and Seamanship.*
26 Anderson, *Oared Fighting Ships.*
27 See Morrison and Coates, *Greek and Roman Oared Warships.*
28 Pliny, VII.207.

29 Livy, XXVIII.30.
30 Polybius, XV.2.
31 Morrison and Coates in *Greek and Roman Oared Warships* opine that they are quinqeremes engaged in a battle of the Punic Wars. No battle is apparent and the scene is one simply of ships on manoeuvre, as could be seen across the Bay from this location. Perhaps, if one wishes, the scene could as well be from the more recent War against the Pirates of 68/67 BC, where such ships were used.
32 From a number of surviving inscriptions.
33 Appian, *The Illyrian Wars* III.
34 Livy, XXIV.35.
35 Livy, XLIV.28.
36 See Torr, *Ancient Ships*.
37 Livy XXXII and XXXV.
38 Lucan, *The Civil War* III.534.
39 Livy, XXXV.26.
40 See Torr, *Ancient Ships*, for an examination of the ancient sources, both as to the number of oars and the duties performed.
41 Polybius, V.62.
42 Livy, XXI.17, describing the forces assigned to the Consul Sempronius in 218 BC.

6

CIVIL WARS
AND IMPERIAL FLEETS:
FIRST CENTURIES BC AND AD

Throughout the second century BC, the Roman fleets were in almost constant action, operating in areas as diverse as the coasts of Portugal, the northern Adriatic and the eastern Mediterranean. All of this activity took its inevitable toll on the ships and crews, which, lacking a dedicated programme of replenishment, by the early first century BC had become neglected and run down. Some successful operations were undertaken but there was no attempt to maintain their previous domination of the seas, leaving a vacuum which was fully exploited by an explosion of piracy throughout the Mediterranean basin. The period of neglect ended in 67 BC, when the fleets were reinvigorated by Gnaeus Pompeius (Pompey the Great) for the war against the fleets of pirates whose depredations had become a plague bringing maritime commerce virtually to a halt. Roman domination of the seas was thereafter imposed and maintained by strong, well-maintained fleets that were kept operational, and piracy disappeared from the Mediterranean for the first time.

The fleets were instrumental in the Civil Wars between Caesar and Pompeius between Octavius and Sextus Pompeius and ultimately between Octavius and Antonius, culminating in the decisive Battle of Actium in 31 BC, where hundreds of ships were engaged.[1] Actium in fact represented the last appearance in action of the great Hellenistic polyreme ships, the *sexteres* and quinquiremes, the latter of which had been the mainstay of Roman fleets for nearly two centuries. For the remainder of this period, the Romans continued to use the same warship types as before, but as the fleets of their enemies were systematically eradicated, they seem to have concentrated more on the lighter types, the larger ships becoming unnecessary and the smaller types being sufficient for the tasks allotted, as well as being more economical.

With the ending of the Civil Wars and the establishment of the Imperial Navy in the twenties BC, Roman hegemony extended over the whole Mediterranean basin. With no enemies left to fight, the Navy's task became to ensure freedom of navigation and the continued suppression of piracy. Apart from a few examples (at least one *sexteres* and a few quinquiremes[2]) the big multi-remes were disposed of, and the quadrireme

Figure 61. Wall painting of two warships from the Temple of Isis at Pompeii, showing the two types of stern referred to in the text.

Figure 62. Wall painting from the Temple of Isis at Pompeii with two more warships, with very prominent oars, the ship on the right appearing to be the larger.

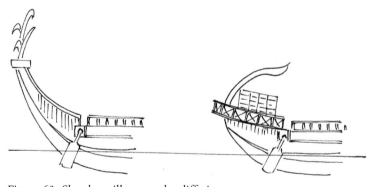

Figure 63. Sketch to illustrate the differing stern types.

and trireme became the biggest types in widespread service, supported by a variety of smaller ships.

With the extension of the Empire and the Augustan settlement of its borders in Europe on the Rhine and Danube, fleets of craft suited to those waters were evolved. Later on, with the invasion and securing of Britain, other types had to be added to cover those northern waters, as well as the responsibilities added by the extension of Roman power into the Black Sea, which, like the Mediterranean, became a Roman lake.

The best contemporary illustrations for the period are the many wall paintings of warships preserved in and recovered from the disastrous eruption of Mount Vesuvius in AD 79. The advantage here is that it took place just across the Bay of Naples from Misenum, the premier naval base of the Empire, established in 22 BC. The artists must have been familiar with the sight of warships and the representations of ships are likely to be more or less accurate. The disadvantage is that they are somewhat stylised, impressions executed quickly to portray an overall effect without great detail. In addition, many of them are now in poor condition. The pictures are also somewhat standardised or formulaic, and it is thus extremely difficult if not almost impossible to discern different types or classes of ship.

Nevertheless, it is still possible to form an impression of these ships and to venture some interpretations. Firstly, all of the ships are shown with decks crammed with marines, armed with round shields and a forest of spears, which must be the simplest and quickest way to portray a crowded deck without providing details of different members of crew or catapults or any other minutiae. None of the ships shows any masts or sailing rig. Two distinct types of stern are consistently shown, one with an open, balustraded deck with a deck cabin and an extended, swept-forward sternpost; these are always shown approaching. The other has a 'closed-in' swept-up stern, topped by an exotic ornament and no cabin; these are always shown going away. This latter stern shape is not unlike earlier, larger types seen in the last chapter. It may be that this was the only way these artists could draw ships, or that they were deliberately trying to indicate two different types – let us hope it was the latter (see Fig. 61 for an example of both).

It would be most convenient to be able to say that the differing types of stern architecture defined different classes of ship, but after examining the forward and aft ends of the depicted oars in 'blocks' on both types, one can only say that the artist put in as many brush strokes as possible to indicate a large number of oars. There was no conscious effort to differentiate biremes or triremes or to accurately portray the actual number of oars. The ends of the oar blocks appear to show what could be either on both approaching and receding ships. At the same time, the 'closed-stern' receding ships do appear to be bigger than the approaching ships in many of the paintings (Fig. 62). If one were to assume that two types were intended to be shown, the receding ships being the bigger triremes and the smaller, approaching ships being biremes, the question then becomes, why were they not also shown in reverse, that is to say, with the biremes going away and the triremes approaching in any of the paintings? The point here is that the one viewed from astern would not look like the other (Fig. 63).

The other thing to note is the uniformity with which these different forms are shown.

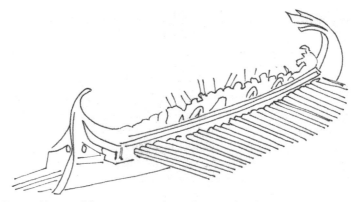

Figure 64. Detail from a mosaic from the Temple of Fortuna at Palestrina, first century BC, showing a bireme warship with the 'closed' type stern.

Figure 65. Detail from a relief showing a monoreme, or at most a bireme, with a 'closed' type stern; probably first century BC.

Figure 66. Fragment of a relief, probably first century AD, showing the prow of a bireme under oar and sail. Note the decoration on the bow and that the stempost has been omitted. (Photograph © the author, image reproduction for non-commercial purposes courtesy the Trustees of the British Museum.)

Thus Figures 61 and 62 and all of the other paintings from the Temple of Isis at Pompeii[3] are matched by an identical convention in paintings at the House of the Vettii and at the Suburban Baths[4] (Figs. 24 and 33), all at Pompeii. Accepting for the moment that the larger ships are triremes, some corroboration can be found in the monument to Cartilius Poplicola at Ostia,[5] which shows a ship with three remes and, although damaged, a 'closed stern'; there are also the examples in the next section (Fig. 67) of the two reliefs of triremes from Pozzuoli, all of the period.

Conversely, and as an exception, a first-century BC mosaic does show a ship with the 'closed stern' approaching, but this is also clearly a bireme (Fig. 64) with a rowing system as outlined in Chapter 2 (see Fig. 18). To further confuse matters, however, Figure 65 shows a ship which is a monoreme, or at the most a bireme, with the 'closed' style of stern. A fragment of a tomb relief (Fig. 66) also shows the bow of a bireme with a sail set upon an artemon. Despite the incongruities thrown up by comparison with the wall paintings, it is valuable evidence that the bireme ships at least were, or could be, fitted with a sailing rig, rather than simply having to take this as an assumption.

Of course, it may well be that all such debate is purely academic and would merely puzzle those ancient artists, who set out to portray 'a warship' *simpliciter*. However, given the proximity of Misenum and the prohibitive costs of housing in the fashionable nearby playgrounds of the Roman super-rich at Baia, Bacoli and Stabia, Pompeii must have been an attractive and reasonable location for retired naval personnel, who would appreciate a nautical theme to their temples and bath houses – hence the frequent recurrence of similar pictures of warships and not of merchant ships. It is logical also that so many of these paintings of ships come from the Temple of Isis, as the Egyptian goddess was popular with seamen as the patron and protector of ships. To her the spring festival, opening the annual sailing season, was dedicated.[6]

TRIREMES

Colour Plate X (Plan 14)
Many tombstones of naval personnel, particularly from the two main Italian fleets at Misenum and Ravenna, have been recovered, and the most commonly referred to ship type on them is the trireme, dozens of names of such ships being recorded.[7] From this it is reasonably safe to infer that triremes of one form or another were in widespread service. It would also appear that the type had evolved from the original (see Chapter 4), as it had lost its role as the mainstay of battle fleets by the mid-third century BC. Thereafter it was used in subsidiary roles where it was no longer required to be the finely tuned ramming machine originally perfected. That is not to say that it could not so act, and as the fastest of the ancient warships, triremes would remain useful as the ancient equivalent of the light cruiser. With the ending of the Civil Wars and the demise of the big multi-remes, it once more became, with the quadrireme, one of the largest of Roman warships.

The present reconstruction is based upon two reliefs of very similar ships from

Figure 67. Two reliefs of the first century BC or AD from Pozzuoli, showing triremes. A structure on the foredeck of the right-hand ship seems unlikely to be a tower but could well portray a catapult. Now in the National Museum, Naples.

Figure 68. Detail from a wall painting at Pompeii, showing a trireme bow with ventilation course and jettied-out top deck and bulwark.

Pozzuoli (ancient Puteoli), dated to the first century BC or AD, and both of the 'closed-stern' type (Fig. 67) and with no stern cabin or overhanging, balustraded rear or poop deck.[8]

Both show stylised warships, again noteworthy, since if they were made locally, their real-life counterparts must have been very familiar to the sculptors. The ships are portrayed with stylised banks of oars, and in the outboard ends of both, features have been formed to indicate that each ship has three remes which have been placed one above the other, presumably for simplicity in carving. Whereas this could be mere decoration on the ship facing left, on the other, the respective layers of oars are rather more staggered in relation to each other, removing any doubt that they are meant to show triremes.

On both ships, men are shown on deck facing aft as if rowing. They are without the helmets, arms and armour with which marines or soldiers are generally shown. Whereas Trajan's Column in Rome does show a warship apparently of three remes, the topmost of which is rowed by men from an upper deck, different considerations apply to that depiction (see Chapter 7). These ships are totally different in overall concept from such later examples, and their relationship to earlier designs, from which they are clearly derived, is obvious. Given their location they must be assumed to be seagoing types. As such these ships follow the armoured tradition and would not leave rowers unprotected on the top deck, which in turns leads us to assume that the men shown on deck are not rowers, who are beneath and protected by a full deck above them.

Both ships give the impression of being solid and heavily built, with similar bow and stern configurations and a heavy wale at the waterline as protection against ram attacks, with another forward and higher up. On both, the hull is foreshortened, exaggerating the depth of hull. The ship facing left has a heavy, vertical bulwark rising above the oars from a position low enough to obscure and thus protect the rowers, and which rises to protect the upper deck.

The steering oars are likewise protected by an aft extension of this structure which is clearly jettied out beyond the hull sides. The bank of oars of the ship facing right is shown emanating from immediately beneath the ship's rail, although the projection of an oar-box is clearly shown, as on the other ship. It seems likely therefore that this is a mistake and the bulwark should be the same as on the ship facing left, the latter being the only configuration that makes sense in interpreting the positions of the rowers.

A topmost (thranite) reme of twenty oars is indicated on one ship and twenty-four on the other. No obvious openings for ventilation are shown in the hull sides, and it is thus assumed that these are hidden by the 'side-screen' bulwarks. On the drawing, therefore, the level between the middle (zygite) and thranite rowers is left as an open framework to give ventilation, yet be impervious to missile attack, protected as it is by the downward projection of the bulwark. The lowest (thalamite) oars are worked through ports in the hull, allowing some 2 feet (610mm) of freeboard. This arrangement means that it is the zygite, rather that the thranite oarsman who has the limited but best view out to the oars of his 'group'.

In view of the heavy build and the added top-weight of a contingent of marines on deck, the hull section should perhaps be comparatively deep and full to avoid tenderness, although the ship would also be somewhat slower. There is a single helmsman on each ship, handling two side rudders with tillers. The ships show detail of balanced rudders, with the area ahead of the blade divided approximately one third and two-thirds fore and aft of the shafts. No stern shelter is shown on either ship, nor any sailing rig, the ship facing right having a pennant staff aft with a cross-tree for displaying a vexillum. However, it is assumed, as always, that a sailing rig could be shipped and a mast-step or tabernacle with securing points for stays and shrouds is included.

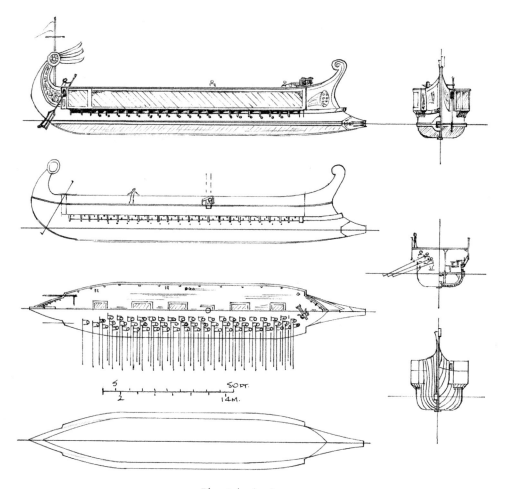

Plan 14. A trireme.

The ship facing left has a strange structure on the foredeck. It does not resemble a tower, but does suggest the front of a catapult or ballista, in which case it is one of extremely few representations of shipboard artillery. Another wall painting (Fig. 68), a three-quarter bow view, shows a trireme and is particularly valuable as it illustrates the overhang of the oar-box and curvature of the bow. Another point to note is that the upper deck is jettied out above the thranite reme to protect the ventilation course, which is clearly shown, and the deck-edge bulwark rises from the outside edge of that course.

One other observation is that with a single (seemingly unprotected) helmsman, these ships would need *c.* 5 foot (1.52m) tillers on their steering oars. The average man's reach is about 4 feet 6 inches (1.37m), thus suggesting a largish turning circle for the ship.

Figure 69. Wall painting from the Temple of Isis at Pompeii showing three warships leaving port.

This need not be taken too literally, as, to improve it, a second helmsman could simply be ordered to take over one of the rudders.

Suggested crew: 5 officers; 6 leading ratings; 10 sailors; 20–25 marines; rowers: 46 thranite, 40 zygite, 36 thalamite; total 168.

Oars: 17 feet (5.2m), gearing 3.25; interscalmium 39 inches (1m)

Dimensions: length overall: 128 feet (39m); waterline: 121 feet (36.9m); beam overall: 21 feet (6.4m); waterline: 16 feet 6 inches (5m); draft: 5 feet 6 inches (1.7m); freeboard: 2 feet (610mm)

LIBURNIANS

Colour Plates XI and XII (Plans 15 and 16)

Another ship type mentioned on many tombstones, as well as in the literature, is the liburnian, probably the best-known name for a type of Roman warship, but for which there is in fact no positive identification. As shown in the last chapter, it is generally accepted that it developed into a bireme warship smaller and lighter than the quadriremes and triremes. The impression is that this type or class of ship became the standard general-purpose light warship of the Roman Navy, none of the other previous designations of light warships continuing in use.[9] That cannot be to say that all liburnians were the same, indeed there are likely to have been wide variations between individual ships and between the liburnians in use in various theatres. For example, as will be seen in the next chapter, both seagoing and river versions seem to have been developed.

Once more the interpretations here are based upon the Pompeii wall paintings, the most plentiful and graphic extant contemporary source. Bearing in mind the reservations that have already been expressed, the open, balustraded stern architecture has been adopted.

Another wall painting (Fig 69) is again of two warships leaving port; a third ship can be made out behind them on the right. As usual, the decks of all the ships are crammed

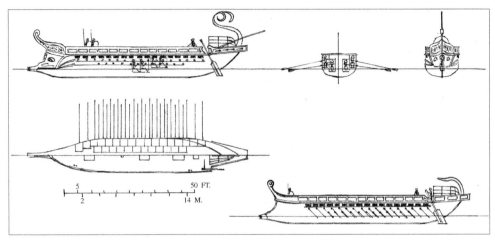

Plan 15. Liburnians.

with men armed with spears and ovoid shields. The two leading ships have similar bow forms, but that behind appears to be different. All three ships have a poop deck over-hanging the stern with a surrounding rail, surmounted by a deck cabin and a sternpost which is swept up and forward, over it.

Both lead ships have the break in the bulwark forward, but also have a very large pillar immediately aft of it and at the forward end of the aft-continuing bulwark. The ship at front right, in particular, displays a foredeck bulwark considerably higher than the rest, and the shields (although not the spears) of the men on deck disappear behind it, suggesting that it is around a raised foredeck. Although such a feature appears later (Chapter 7) and has already been considered in relation to quadriremes (Chapter 5), some corroboration of it for this period is needed before assuming it here, in use on a liburnian.

The oars of both leading ships emerge *en masse* from beneath what appears to be a ventilation course. Upon closer examination, one could almost say that it is in fact an oar-box, with the top reme emerging from it and the lower from beneath it. As we have seen, such an arrangement would work well for a bireme, even if not strictly necessary, but in view of the impressionistic nature of these paintings, this would be to read too much accuracy into them (the statue apparently rising over the stempost of the right-hand ship is in fact atop a pillar behind it). Accordingly the ships in the foreground of this painting (similar as they are to the other paintings in the series) are interpreted as smallish bireme warships, namely liburnians.

The original drawing (Plan 15) and model emerged as a modest ship of 58 oars, 85 feet (25.9m) overall. It was completed in the ornate manner, as suggested by some of the paintings, for duty perhaps as a station ship at Misenum, for ceremonial duties and escorting the Imperial families (Augustus and Caligula had villas nearby, and Tiberius famously lived on Capri), rather than for combat use further afield. The other drawing

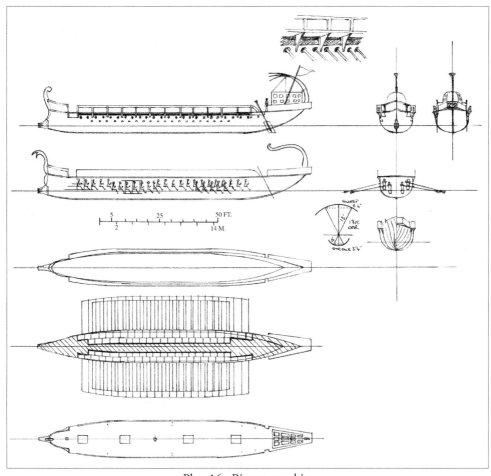

Plan 16. Bireme warship.

and models are of the more austere, active-service version of the same ship, increased to sixty oars. A detachable sailing rig is assumed as before, carried on crutches when not in use.

Suggested crew: 4 officers; 6 sailors; 10 marines; 6 archers; 60 rowers, 34 in the upper reme, 26 in the lower: total 86.

Dimensions: length overall: 85 feet (25.9m); waterline: 76 feet (23m); beam overall: 12 feet 6 inches (3.8m); waterline: 11 feet (3.35m); draft: 3 feet (915mm); freeboard: 2 feet (610mm).

A different interpretation is provided by the next drawing (Plan 16) and model, an attempt to contrive a larger, more powerful and longer-ranging ship, but still basing the design on the wall paintings. Accordingly, dimensions have been increased, allowing for additional rowers, eighty-eight now being accommodated. The after deck has a shelter or cabin, probably a light wooden framework or wicker frames with a cover, perhaps leather or canvas.

No oar-box is shown clearly, as previously mentioned, and indeed is hardly necessary for the ships, but the proximity of the bottom of the bulwark and top of the 'oar-box' suggests a jettied-out deck edge, to shelter a row of ventilation ports.

Model crew: 3 officers; 6 sailors; 24 marines; 48 upper reme and 40 lower reme rowers: total 121.

Dimensions: length overall: 117 feet (35.66m); waterline: 105 feet (32m); beam overall: 16 feet (4.9m); waterline: 13 feet (3.96m); draft: 3 feet 6 inches (1.05m); freeboard: 2 feet (610mm).

Oars: 17 feet (5.2m), gearing 3.25.

SCOUTS. 'EXPLORATORIAE'. 'SPECULATORIAE'

Colour Plate XIII (Plan 17)

It is not clear if this was a specialised type of vessel or the title given to any ship so employed. There are no known representations that can be positively identified as such. The designation is known from the first century BC onwards.

The reconstruction here is based upon a wall painting from Rome of the first century BC, showing three people in a very ornate rowing boat (Fig. 70). The boat is clearly modelled on warship fashion, even having vestigial stern gangways by way of decoration, which appear to be resting on a bracket. There is little deck sheer and it seems to have the 'closed' style of stern previously discussed. If the figures are not shown oversize, the steering oar is superfluous, and the boat will scale to approximately 25 feet (7.6m) in length. Mosaics from Tunisia of rather later date (second and third centuries AD) give further examples of small boats made after the fashion of warships (Fig. 71) which can, perhaps, provide some corroboration, or at least show that it was a more widespread practice, as well as long-lived. As further corroboration, Figure 72 shows a detail from a grave stela from northern Greece with a boat of very similar form.

For the underwater shape, guidance has been sought from the small ships at the Ostia Museum, which exhibit a bow shape that would fit well on a modern powerboat, being fine and well shaped for speed. The remains of a small boat at Herculaneum display similar lines (first century AD, but could be slightly earlier). Accordingly, the drawing is intended to show a light scouting craft with fine lines and shallow draft. This boat was evolved at a time of widespread piracy, and with marines as rowers, rather than a separate rowing crew, could have been useful for 'gunboat diplomacy' in such areas with short sea passages as the Dalmatian and Greek islands, as well as being the eyes of the fleet.

It has light rig in view of the shallow draft, mounted on crutches when not in use, and twenty oars. One side rudder should be sufficient, but a second is carried as a spare. The ram is more for show than intent, and with the benefit of hindsight and having

Figure 70. Small, open pleasure boat from a wall painting from Rome, first century AD, now in the Museo Nazionale, Romano, after Casson.

Figure 71. Examples of small boats, made in the fashion of warships. Details from second- and third-century AD mosaics from Tunisia.

made a scale crew, slightly more generous proportions as to length and beam would have been preferred.

Suggested crew: 1 junior officer; 2 leading ratings; 20 rowers: total 23.

Dimensions: length overall: 48 feet (14.6m); waterline: 44 feet (13.4m); beam overall: 6 feet 6 inches (2m); waterline: 6 feet (1.83m); draft: 18 inches (457mm); freeboard: 2 feet 3 inches (685mm); length-to-beam ratio 8:1.

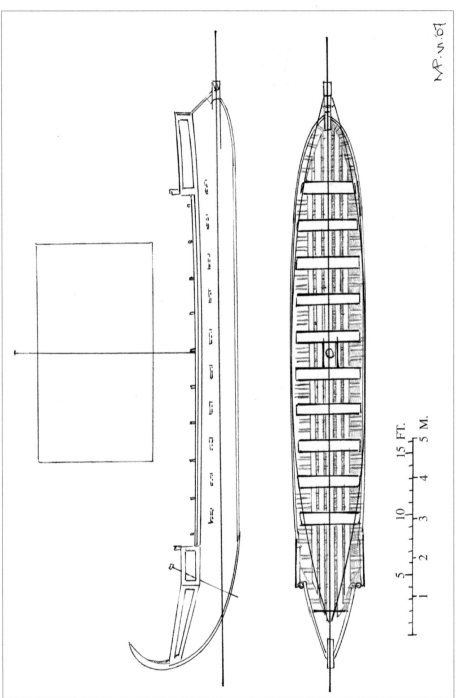

15 FT.

5 M.

Plan 17. Scout ship.

N.P. v. 61

RIVER CRAFT

A totally different, specialised type of craft was developed for use on the rivers of central Europe which, apart from their method of construction, bore no relationship to the seagoing types thus far considered. Two examples of these boats were discovered at the site of the Roman fort at Oberstimm, near Ingolstadt in Bavaria. The boats date to the period from late in the reign of Domitian (AD 81–96) to mid-way into that of Trajan (AD 98–117) and are from a location close to the point at which the *Limes*, which enclosed the territory of the Rhine–Danube re-entrant (the *Agri Decumates*), joined the Danube.[10]

Their date coincides with the completion of the Roman move into this area, and their location on the Upper Danube places them in the province of Rhaetia and under the command of the *Classis Pannonica*. This was the Roman river fleet for the Danube from its source to the Iron Gates Gorge (approximately 100 miles or 160km east of Belgrade). The genesis of these boats may well be earlier, as the Romans had a flotilla of boats on the River Sava when, from 16 BC, Augustus ordered the advance of Roman territory, first to the parallel River Drava, then to establish his new border on the Danube itself. In all of these successive moves, the original flotilla was augmented and used, forming an essential part of the machinery of conquest, both supporting the troops with offensive action and keeping them supplied. The flotilla was finally and formally constituted into the *Classis Pannonica* in 12 BC, when the final border was established on the Danube.

These two boats were both built using the traditional Mediterranean methods of shell-first construction (Chapter 1) with mortice and tenon joints securing the hull planking, edge-to-edge. They are open, monoreme craft with every man aboard as a combatant, rather than the separate rowing and marine contingents found on the larger, seagoing ships. They are both about 51 feet (15.4m) overall length and about 9 feet (2.7m) beam and rowed by 16 to 20 oars, one man per oar, and also having a light, stowable rig. The hulls are very shallow, only 3 feet 3 inches (1m) from keel to bulwark and thus probably drawing no more than a foot (305mm), suiting them to working in smaller rivers and tributaries.

On the Lower Danube (from the Iron Gates downriver) there is evidence (see Chapter 7) to show that larger, heavier warships, more akin to their seagoing equivalents, were deployed and that this also occurred on the Rhine, at least from its middle reaches downwards. With such large ships operating in concert with these light craft, a two-tier approach to riverine warships is suggested, these lighter, open craft for patrols, interdiction and penetration up smaller channels and tributaries, backed and supported by the heavier ships for patrolling the main channels.[11] That this was so is attested by the historian Tacitus, writing c. AD 100, of the revolt of Civilis on the Rhine in AD 69: 'He manned all the biremes and single-banked [sic.] vessels he had and to these was added a large number of small craft carrying thirty or forty men apiece and fitted out like liburnians.' Whether the *Classis Pannonica* also deployed larger ships is not known, but it seems likely. The river is certainly big enough, and although a comparatively peaceful sector of the border in the early Empire, it was subject to occasional violent

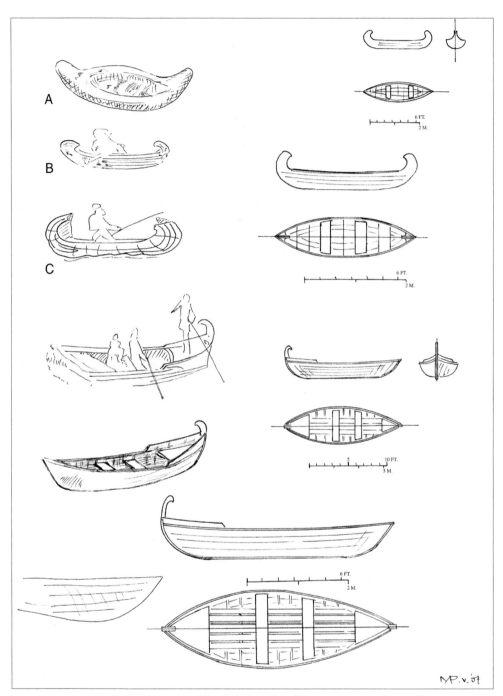

Plan 18.　Small craft.

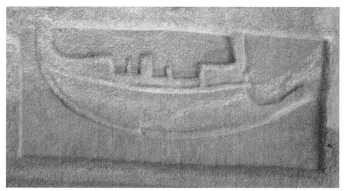

Figure 72. Detail from a grave stela at Dion, northern Greece

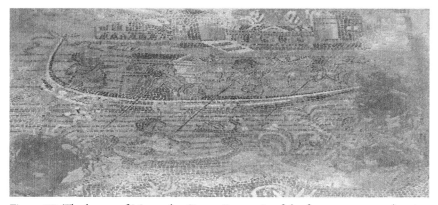

Figure 73. The house of Menander, Pompeii, mosaic of the first century AD, showing in the foreground a small open boat shaped like a canoe, with upturned bow and stern and single occupant who appears to be paddling.

irruptions from the other side (as in AD 85). The general type of smaller river warship was to remain in service, with some evolution, especially as to building method, for centuries to come (see Chapter 8).

SMALL CRAFT, TENDERS AND SHIP'S BOATS

Colour Plate XIV (Plan 18)
The 'canoe'-shaped boat (Fig. 73), of a type known only to be shown with a single occupant, is interpreted as a very small open boat, suitable as a tender to the smaller warship types. The form is extremely old and apparently widespread, similar examples being known from Egypt, Greece and Italy. It could well, of course, be a type of coracle

Figure 74. Small fishing boat with a man in the stern standing on a raised platform, sculling or poling the boat while two others are rowing or working nets. Bow is indistinct as a result of damage but appears bluff. Detail from a wall painting at the Suburban Baths, Pompeii.

of skin or waterproofed canvas over a light frame. Examples on the drawing (Plan 18) are (A) a clay model from Mycenae, *c.* 1200 BC;[12] (B) extract from a mosaic at Pompeii (Fig. 73);[13] and (C) a detail from another mosaic, of the first century BC.[14]
Suggested dimensions: length 9 feet (2.7m); beam 2 feet 6 inches (760mm).

Figure 74 shows a small boat based upon a wall painting at Pompeii, one man steering or sculling, standing on a stern platform.[15] Another man rows, seated on a thwart, and a third, somewhat indistinct, is also perhaps rowing. The painting has deteriorated around the bow and therefore a form has been adopted, based upon a small boat hull at Herculaneum; similar, later bow forms can be found on boats in the museum at Ostia. On the lower drawing of Plan 18, the sketch is from the wall painting; that below it, the reconstruction; and the lower is of the bow form from Herculaneum.
Dimensions: length 15 feet (4.57m); beam 5 feet (1.52m).

NOTES

1   Pitassi, *The Navies of Rome.*
2   The continued existence of these ships is confirmed by their being mentioned on tombstones of the early Imperial period.

3 These are the best preserved of the wall paintings of ships and are now in the Museum at Naples, where they have been restored and cleaned.

4 Of the others, the House of the Vettii has been closed for some years for conservation; those in the Suburban Baths are still in situ.

5 This prominent monument is outside the Marine Gate at Ostia Antica.

6 Pitassi, *The Navies of Rome.*

7 The lists, with addenda, are related in Morrison and Coates, *Greek and Roman Oared Warships.*

8 The original reliefs are in the National Museum, Naples.

9 Tombstones of naval personnel of the imperial period, in many cases specify the deceased's ship by type as well as by name. For a listing, see Morrison and Coates, *Greek and Roman Oared Warships.* A good, recent (2005) example is the grave stela discovered near Ravenna, where the incumbent is described as 'Captain and Optio of the Liburnian Aurata'.

10 Austin and Rankov, *Exploratio.*

11 Tacitus, *The Histories*, V.23.

12 After Johnston, *Ship and Boat Models in Ancient Greece.*

13 In the House of Menander, Pompeii.

14 Mosaic of a Nile scene from the Palazzo Barberini, after Casson, *Ships and Seafaring in Ancient Times.*

15 Wall painting in the Suburban Baths at Pompeii.

7

HEIGHT OF EMPIRE: SECOND AND THIRD CENTURIES AD

Throughout the second and for most of the third centuries AD, Roman domination of the seas was totally unchallenged, and the policing of the Empire's sea and river ways, while requiring considerable numbers, was a routine for which existing types of warship were perfectly adequate. With no enemies to confront, the duties of the fleets of the Mediterranean and Black Seas were limited to patrols to ensure that piracy did not occur, for the fast transport of important personnel and dispatches and to intervene and transport troops to deal with any revolt or threat that might arise. On the river frontiers, constant patrols were maintained to control the flow of peoples and goods across them and especially to ensure that all fees and taxes on river traffic were levied and paid. On the northern coasts of Europe, the most important duty was to maintain the military communications link between Britannia and the mouth of the Rhine and their respective garrisons, as well as the more routine coastal patrols.

It would seem that the types larger than a trireme went out of use, probably by the mid- to late second century AD as they are no longer attested. For the second century, the major activity was on the Danube, for Trajan's (AD 98–117) Dacian Wars between AD 101 and 106 and the wars of Marcus Aurelius (AD 161–80) across the Danube, both of which are commemorated on their respective extant columns in Rome, which give the best and mostly accurate representations of the types of ship used. To reinforce his river fleets, Trajan especially, brought seagoing ships up the Danube from the Black Sea to support his campaigns upon that river and its tributaries. His successor, Hadrian (AD 117–38), the only emperor to travel to all of his provinces, went a lot of the way by sea and was certainly conveyed by warship for some of that time (see Fig. 81).

For the third century AD, there survive virtually no representations of warships, and from the death of Caracalla in AD 217, the Empire plunged into a series of crises, lasting seventy years, that nearly ended it. The continual necessity and cost of keeping as large an army as possible in the field, meant that the Roman fleets were neglected and run-down and the great Imperial fleets became a shadow of their former selves. Towards the end of the period, control of the Black Sea was lost and barbarian sea raiders, in increasing numbers and proficiency, penetrated even into the Aegean. There was in addition a resurgence of piracy. In the north, barbarian seafaring abilities also improved and increased. Their early, tentative voyages along north European coasts had developed, by the very end of the period, to include the capability of making open sea crossings.[1]

In the early part of this period, Roman warships had evolved to deal with the roles required of them in the long period of comparative peace and stability since Actium in 31 BC. Although the larger, earlier types were no longer needed, ships in service were of a level sufficient to give them superiority over any barbarian craft likely to be met, details of which Roman intelligence gathering and the capture of examples would provide.[2] Even later, during the period of crisis for the Empire of the latter third century AD, it was the neglect and run-down of the Navy's formations, with the consequent reduction in activity, that allowed barbarian raids, rather than any inherent weakness in Roman ships or seafaring ability.

TRAJAN'S SHIPS

In one scene on Trajan's Column (LXXIX and LXXX)[3] three types of ship are apparently shown (Fig 75). In the foreground, what appears to be a *liburna,* rowed at two levels; in the rear another bireme, this time of an apparently heavier build altogether and with a sailing rig stowed on crutches. In the centre is a trireme, clearly shown being rowed at three levels. All three types show a strong family resemblance. Of the two biremes it would seem that the front (lighter-looking) one is a riverine craft, while the rearmost, heavier-looking one could represent a seagoing version.[4] The inclusion of the two types together is reasonable, as warships were drafted from the seagoing fleets to bolster the Danube flotillas for the invasion. All of these ships do, however, show a significant change from previous types and have evolved in a service that had by now long confronted no opposing navies. No longer threatened by opponents with rams, the heavy waterline wales/armour have been dispensed with. The ram has changed in the manner noted earlier, and the centre portion of the hull over the rowers is not so heavily built or even necessarily covered or decked-over. Since their opponents had no artillery, light screening hung on the open side panels and perhaps overhead, appears to have been sufficient protection against arrows or javelins. The forward sections of the ships have, however, become heavier and more complex and are obviously intended as the principal fighting areas. Note that the gap forward in the bulwark for the boarding bridge or gangway is retained on the trireme, blocked by a removable drop-in panel (Fig. 76).

All three ships, in common with the other warships shown on Trajan's Column (XXXIII and XXXVI[5]) are shown being rowed by men on the open top decks, using oars over and through the bulwark screens, as well as by the oars of lower remes, protruding conventionally through the hull sides. Given the artistic convention of showing figures oversize in relation to the ships, it is difficult to judge the accuracy of the operations depicted. It is for this reason that the scenes are generally interpreted as illustrating

Figure 75. Trajan's ships. Scene from his column showing a trireme and two biremes.

crewmen that would not in fact have been visible (and vulnerable). This was simply another conventional way to show that the men were aboard the ships. For that reason, artistic licence is assumed to have been applied and the rowers were in reality behind the screens and rowing through 'proper' oar-ports.

The worrying thing about such an interpretation is that, although convenient, it must be assumed that artists actually went on the Dacian expeditions and made sketches and recorded details which were later used to plan and sculpt the panels of the column. That this is so is self-evident from the wealth of fine detail incorporated into every aspect of the work. Having taken so much trouble to include details of every item shown, to a far greater extent than would ever be seen by a viewer standing beneath the column, it would be curious that they had made a fundamental error in depicting the warships by showing them in any form other than that in which they appeared, notwithstanding the exaggeration in figure sizes.

This being so, and accepting that a warship would not normally be rowed in such an apparently ad hoc fashion over and through the deck side screens, alternative scenarios have to be considered.

All of the ships are shown crammed with men and being used for trooping (although none are shown in armour, with weapons or even helmets), which is the context of their inclusion in the reliefs. Strangely, officers and helmsmen (also without armour, weapons, and so on) are shown at the sterns, but the foredecks are unmanned. Supposing that some of the men on deck have been issued with spare oars to 'lend a hand' and offset their weight on board by augmenting the regular rowing crews, rowing as best they can from the upper deck, the question arises as to what they are sitting on. Perhaps they are kneeling. In either event, it does not work as a serious proposition. Further, against what are they plying their oars, since no tholes or securing for the oars, necessary if they are to be worked, are shown. Bearing in mind the trouble that was taken and the practice

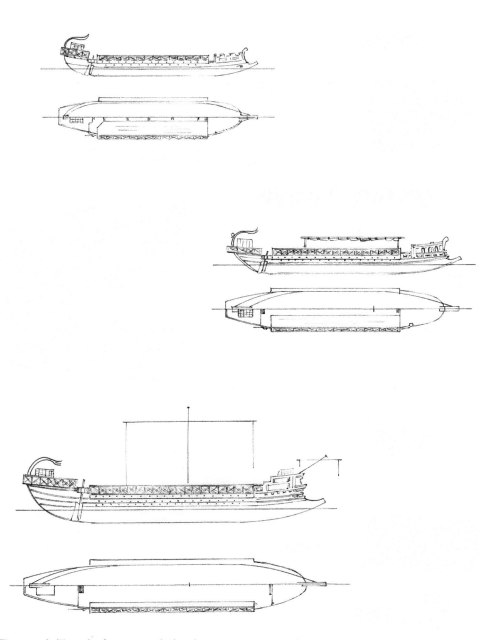

Figure 76. Trajan's ships. Initial sketches, to constant scale, to extract and analyse the three distinct warship types in the panel of the column shown in Figure 75; at the top, the river liburnian; in the centre, the seagoing version; at the bottom, the trireme.

necessary to train rowing crews, the addition of a few ad hoc soldiers with oars could only prove disruptive, at the least. Finally, sitting upon an all-enclosing top deck puts those men's tholes (assuming that they have them) in the order of 5 feet (1.52m) above those of the lower reme, i.e. not in accordance with the reliefs and which would cause them to be incapable of operation, being at too acute an angle.

If, however, one accepts for the moment the temporary nature of the deck 'crews', the ships themselves could then be viewed differently, as two monoremes and a bireme. The monoremes thus become the same in format as the (later) Rhine patrol ship (see Chapter 8), although the distinction between them could remain, i.e. light and heavy versions. The 'trireme' then becomes a bireme, again of seagoing type, from its highly built-up forecastle, artemon with sail rigged and even the seahorse motif on the bow. However, the geometry of such a layout fails to meet one of the essential criteria previously expounded, namely that it does not work in practice and, at the same time, accord with the reliefs. Further, the ships are foreshortened to show only a few oars, half a dozen or so, to fit them into the medium. There would have been many more in reality, so the 'mistake' theory would on balance appear to be the most likely. The manner of depicting the 'deck crews' oversize in such a way that they were visible, forced upon the sculptors, has led to this distortion.

RIVER 'LIBURNA'. 'CLASSIS MOESICA'

Colour Plate XVII (Plan 19)
The ship in the foreground of the 'three-ship panel' of Trajan's Column is also the most commonly shown type of warship on the column, repeated many times, with only small variations. This ship is of the lighter, smaller type and thus interpreted as a specialised version of the liburnian, evolved to be most suitable for riverine operations. As in all of the renditions, the crew is shown oversize on deck, rowing in an ad hoc manner through or over the side screens and without tholes; a second reme is shown emerging from below the screen construction. None of this type is shown with a sailing rig (Fig. 77).

In interpreting these scenes, once again, one has to assume that the artist was familiar with and sought to accurately portray the ship (there is enough detail and the proportions shown look sufficiently 'right' to justify this) but had to compromise in that he was required to show a crew (oversize) and one that was rowing. As they seem to have no other purpose, the side screens are presumably there to protect the rowing crew, who by extension would therefore in reality sit behind them, not above them. In exaggerating the size of the crewmen, the artist can show only a few of these very oversize figures on what would otherwise be an amazingly and unnecessarily complex vessel to carry so few men. This is reflected also in the tiny number of oars shown, typically seven or eight per side. The compromise has clearly led to oars shown emerging over and through the screens at all manner of levels.

If it is accepted that a bireme is intended and that the oars of the upper reme, like the lower, must emerge at the same level, it seems most logical to put their oar-ports

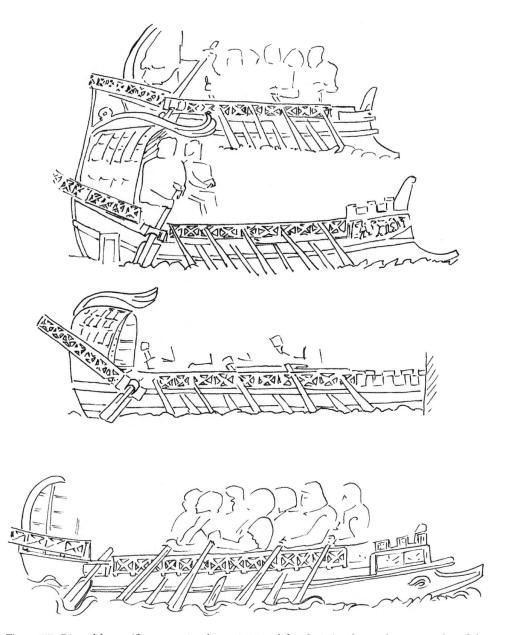

Figure 77. River *liburna* (figures omitted or minimised for clarity). Above: three examples of the type after Trajan's Column. All are rowed as biremes and show the mounting bracket for the starboard side rudder. Below: the ship at the front of the scene in Figure 75 and the top in Figure 76.

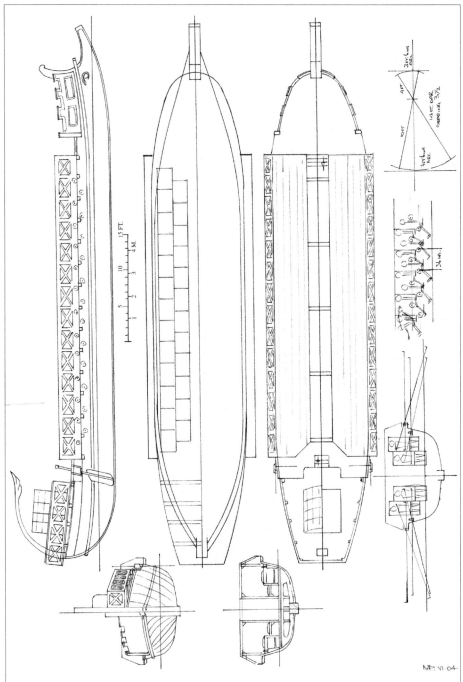

Plan 19. River *liburna*.

along the lower edge of the side screens, so that these men can have the benefit of their protection.

The drawing emerged well and looking 'right' in comparison with the original. However, in the making of the model hull and having fitted the tholes and seats for the lower reme oarsmen, all of which went in and fitted perfectly, when it came to fitting the seats, footrests and tholes for the upper reme, it was quickly found that if made according to the drawing then the lower rowers would have insufficient room in which to row and, indeed, could not do so without fouling the upper reme. A great deal of juggling with cut-outs of the inboard arc of the oars and a cone carved to represent the operation of the loom of the oar led to the upper oarsmen's seats having to be raised a scale 9 inches (228mm) and the staggering of their seats being changed. This in turn led to the jettying outboard of their tholes having to be increased so that they did not keep hitting their knees when rowing. The overhang of the outrigger from which the upper oars are worked does now appear a little excessive when compared to the original, but it must be borne in mind that the latter is a bas or low relief and not accurate in depth, and had to be compressed and foreshortened to only a few inches as well as adjusted to the curved surface of the column.

The proportions shown for this type, such as the relative height of the bulwarks to the length, seem to indicate a ship of modest size, rowed as a bireme, with an open fighting platform forward and a raised poop deck jettied out over the stern with a small shelter upon it. The side rudders, of which two are assumed, are secured by brackets and mounted lower than the poop deck and at the level of the upper reme. The ships have a longish, upward turning ram, presumably suited to dealing with the lighter and open enemy craft. The same pattern of side screens is shown on all of them, covering the midships section and thus the rowers. Presumably in action this could be covered by thick leather screens. The figures are shown seated, and on the basis of this and the seemingly modest dimensions of the ship, no deck over the rowers was fitted. To counter the effect of plunging missiles, some form of light protective screening over the rowers would have been provided which could additionally provide shelter from inclement weather. A few light spars were therefore fitted at intervals along the top edges of and between the side screens to carry such awnings and also to maintain the separation and give stiffness to the screens themselves.

In the light of such considerations, it seemed not unreasonable to define the ship as a bireme of fifty oars, which proved possible while at the same time allowing the resulting drawing to 'look right' and in accordance with what was shown on the column. One omission from the drawing is the lack of thwarts in the main body of the hull, the rowing area, to prevent the hull sides from splaying. It would be possible to introduce some at the level of the lower reme seats, which should be sufficient to stiffen the hull. Incidentally, there is absolutely no evidence linking the much-used name 'liburnian' with any of these ships, but insofar as a *liburna* was a light(ish) bireme warship,[6] it seems an appropriate and tolerable permissible liberty.

Suggested crew: 2 officers; 4 sailors; 10 marines; 26 upper reme rowers; 24 lower reme rowers; total crew: 66.

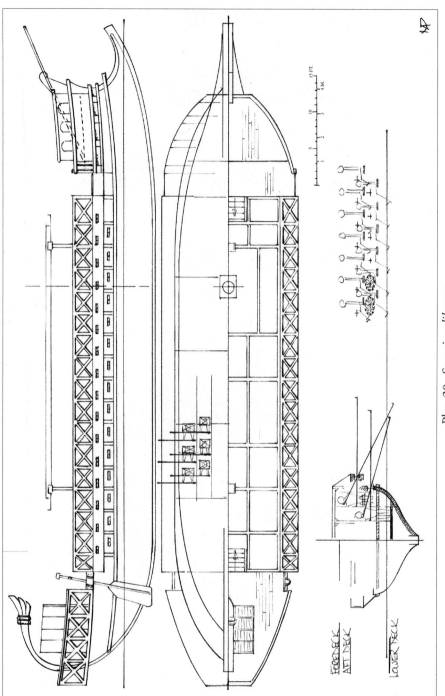

FORE DECK
AFT DECK

LOWER DECK

15 FT.
10
5
4 M.
3
2
1

Plan 20. Seagoing *liburna*.

Figure 78. The seagoing *liburna*, showing the built-up forecastle and rigged artemon (after Trajan's Column).

Dimensions: length overall: 75 feet (22.8m); waterline: 71 feet (21.6m); beam overall: 15 feet (4.57m); waterline: 12 feet (3.66m); draft: 2 feet 6 inches (762mm); freeboard: 18 inches (457mm).
Oars: 14 feet (4.26m) at a gearing of 3.5.

SEAGOING 'LIBURNA', EARLY SECOND CENTURY AD

(Plan 20)
Similar in overall concept, but altogether bigger and more heavily built than the river version, this is a seagoing craft which has evolved considerably from its early Imperial predecessors. Once again, the liberty is taken of classifying this ship as a liburnian, although there is no firm evidence to confirm that it is indeed such. Apart from the change in the form of the ram, previously noted, it has also dispensed with the waterline protective wales. Also gone is the completely decked-over 'armoured' box of the rowing crew, the ships now having an open deck with the provision of side screens and frames for the rigging of awnings and protective covers, sufficient protection against enemies with no artillery.

The underwater hull cross-section is finer and deeper, with a concave deadrise from the keel. This is possible as dispensing with the covering upper deck and bulwarks, together with their crew and marines, has considerably reduced the top-weight which demanded the greater balancing displacement of earlier hulls. As distinct from the flatter-bottomed river ship, this hull form is evolved for sea use and to give better stability, especially when under sail. There is also increased freeboard and a well has been left clear around the mainmast (which, on reflection, could be moved aft by about 4 feet/1.22m) to enable handling of the rig.

Another big difference from the earlier ships is in the forward section, where an altogether higher and more massive structure has been developed. As for the river version, the foredeck has become, especially with the lack of an overall covering top deck, the principal fighting platform of the ship. Unable to carry a tower, the foredeck has been raised to give a height advantage and as a bonus, to help divert bow waves and make the ship less prone to being wet forward. In short, a structure that would later be called the forecastle. From the relief, beam ends are visible below the foredeck, suggesting that the fighting platform is jettied out to make it broader right forward. There is now room below the foredeck for a small cabin with good headroom. Together with the small cabin below the poop deck, there is room for stowage of provisions and supplies which would enable the ship to undertake longer patrols. Aft, the ship is steered by conventional side rudders but operated from poop-deck level, i.e. higher than in the river version. With reference to earlier observations, thwarts have been introduced to stiffen the hull at the lower reme seat level, the highest possible point while avoiding fouling the rowers.

Assuming, as before, that the outrigger for the upper reme projects 21 inches (533mm) beyond the hull sides proper, and as the rowing forces operate against their outboard edges, then some support is desirable. None is obvious, but in some views of the reliefs from different angles, details do appear which could well indicate the presence of such supports, between the third, fourth and fifth oars from the bow. Bracing knees, led to the wale below, are thus introduced. A gangway or boarding bridge can be stowed athwartships forward, between the oarbox and the raised foredeck platform.

The ship is shown on the panel with a mast, sail and yard stowed on crutches, establishing that it carried a full sailing rig, which could be stowed when not in use. On another panel (LXXXVI) a similar ship is shown with an artemon and foresail rigged (Fig. 78). As it emerged, the ship looks well in accordance with the relief, but with only sixty-two oars is possibly under-powered. The shaded areas on the rowing layout are to indicate the maximum travel of the lower oars, where they pass beneath and to clear the upper rowers above.

Suggested crew: 3 officers; 6 sailors; 15 marines; 32 upper reme rowers; 30 lower reme rowers; total crew: 86.

Dimensions: length overall: 90 feet (27.4m); waterline: 81 feet (24.7m); beam overall: 18 feet 6 inches (5.64m); waterline: 13 feet 4 inches (4.06m); draft 4 feet 6 inches (1.37m); freeboard 2 feet (609mm).

Oars 15 feet (4.57m), gearing 3.3; operated at 26 and 15 degrees.

'TRAJAN'S TRIREME'

Colour Plate XVIII (Plan 21)
The largest of the three ships under review is that in the centre, in use as the Emperor's flagship. It is very similar in overall concept and style to the other two ships in company with it, but two remes are clearly shown emerging from below the lattice-work side screens. One reme emerges from the space between the two hull wales and the upper

from between the upper wale and the screening. The thranite or topmost oars are apparently being plied through the screens once more and the previous observations in that regard are again applicable.

Although possibly the result of the constraints of the panel size used, there is little difference in the relative sizes of the trireme and the seagoing liburnian behind it. We must assume that the former was in fact larger and had considerably more oars than the notional few shown.

Aft, the side rudder is omitted as hidden by the ship in the foreground, but otherwise, is the same in concept as the others, only larger. There is what appears to be a lantern hanging from the sternpost decoration. Such a device was used to indicate a flagship in the Second Punic War (218–202 BC), where three were used for a night voyage and may be serving a similar purpose here.[7] The foredeck structure is altogether more massive again and can genuinely be regarded as a forecastle. It seems to be a most complex construction, with at least two levels and topped by an artemon with a small sail rigged; no yard is clearly marked, but must be assumed, as must the rigging for it. Once more, beam ends can be seen below the forecastle, indicating that extra width for the fighting platform has been gained by jettying it outboard. The built-up part forward could indicate a raised central portion in lieu of a tower, of perhaps 10 feet × 5 feet (3 × 1.5m), leaving two flanking platforms of approximately 14 feet × 5 feet (4.3 × 1.5m) at foredeck level. Such a raised platform, while giving archers an advantage, could also explain the apparent smallness of the artemon with its sail, compared to the size of the more realistically shown rig stowed on the ship behind (the seagoing *liburna*). Unlike that ship, apart from the artemon, no rig is shown and presumably has been landed. If shipped, it could also be stowed when not in use, on removable crutches. Although there is no high stempost as previously, the whole bow area seems highly decorated with relief work , possibly in carved and painted wood.

The gap in the bulwark for the boarding bridge or gangway is indicated but has been closed with a (presumably) drop-in weather board or panel. The topmost level of the forecastle has been finished with crenellations and marked to resemble stonework. No mainmast is shipped, but a full rig as part of the ship's seagoing equipment can be assumed from the presence of the artemon.

Dimensions of the original sketch were for a ship of 114 feet (34.7m) overall length and 110 oars. As the concept developed, however, and detail drawings were made to establish the relative positions of the remes of rowers, it was found with the initial layout that the thranite oars were at an more acute angle than desirable, that the thalamite oars fouled those of the zygites above them and that provision had to be made (in the absence of a structural top deck) for thwarts within the hull. These ends were achieved by adjusting the relative heights of the remes and canting their seats slightly outboard and also increasing the interscalmium to 4 feet (1.22m). To accommodate thwarts, the interscalmium was increased by a further foot (305mm) between every third rower; this all increased the length of the 'engine room' to 86 feet (26.2m). Oars of 14 feet 6 inches (4.42m) are at a slightly higher gearing of 3.6, but still within acceptable limits (Fig. 79).

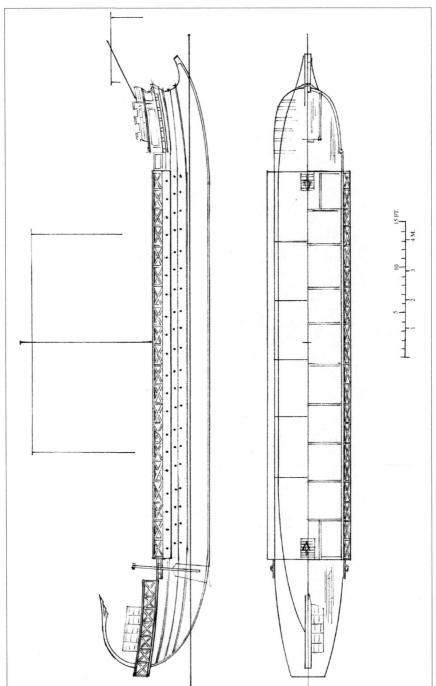

Plan 21. Trireme.

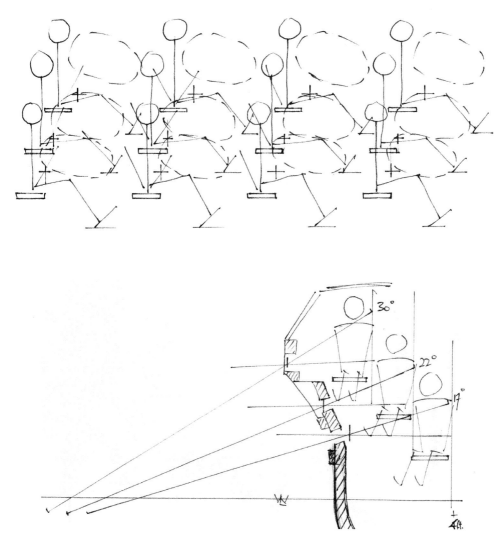

Figure 79. Trireme rowing system analysis.

Suggested crew: 4 officers; 10 sailors; 20 marines; 40 thranite rowers; 40 zygite rowers; 40 thalamite rowers; total crew: 154.

Final dimensions: length overall: 138 feet (42m); waterline: 122 feet (37.2m); beam overall: 19 feet (5.8m); waterline: 14 feet (4.3m); draft: 4 feet 6 inches (1.4m); freeboard: 2 feet (610mm)

Oars: 14 feet 6 inches (4.42m), operated at 30, 22 and 17 degrees.

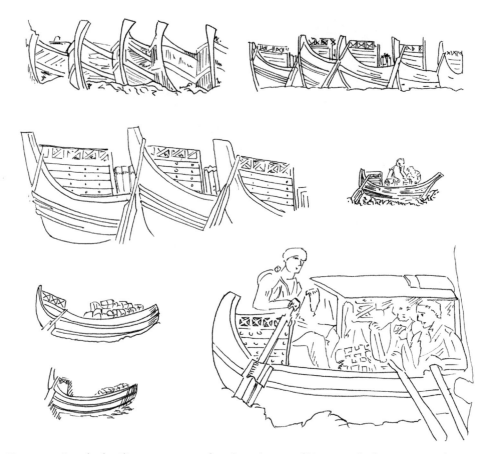

Figure 80. Standard military transport after the columns of Trajan and of Marcus Aurelius. Top row: bows and sterns where the ships are being used as pontoons for bridging. Centre row: left, details of stern cabins; right, with a different style of stempost. Bottom row: left, two being used to carry freight; right, being rowed across the bulwark and with an awning over the centre part (note heavy bracket for mounting the steering oar).

MILITARY (RIVER) TRANSPORTS, SECOND CENTURY AD

Colour Plate XIX (Plan 22)

A standardised type of military transport appears in common use on the Danube. Shown in use as pontoons for bridging rivers and as cargo transport ships on both Trajan's Column (erected in AD 113, to commemorate his Dacian Wars of AD 102–6) and Marcus Aurelius' Column (erected shortly after his death in AD 180). They were thus in service as a type for at least the best part of a century (Figure 80).

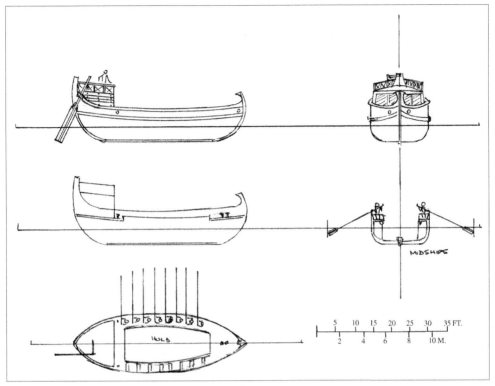

Plan 22. Military transport.

They were obviously mass-produced to a standard design, which included a facility for supporting bridging. As to size, the illustrations of bridges show men marching three and four abreast and also with horses abreast of the men; assuming a width of, say, 3 feet (914mm) per man carrying his equipment or for a riderless horse and a width of perhaps 12 feet (3.65m) plus a foot (305mm) or so either side for the width of the roadway, we have a total of some 14–15 feet (4.26 to 4.57m). If this was laid across the midships third of the length of the hulls of the ships, a total length of about 48 feet (14.63m) results. To make the ship broad but as shallow of draft as possible for river use, say 3:1, gives a beam of 16 feet (4.87m) and a draft of 3 feet (914mm) empty with a flat bottom and a capacity of up to perhaps 30 tons of cargo. The representations indicate that the hull was formed into a ship-like, double-ended bow and stern, rather than bluff- or blunt-ended, like a barge or lighter.

No rig is shown and the ships were thus rowed or pulled by tow ropes. A single steering oar is shown hung from the starboard quarter and operated from a poop deck with a rail, atop a stern cabin mounted on the main deck. Under oars, a single reme operated across the bulwark of eight or so men a side each pulling a 17 feet (5.2m) oar

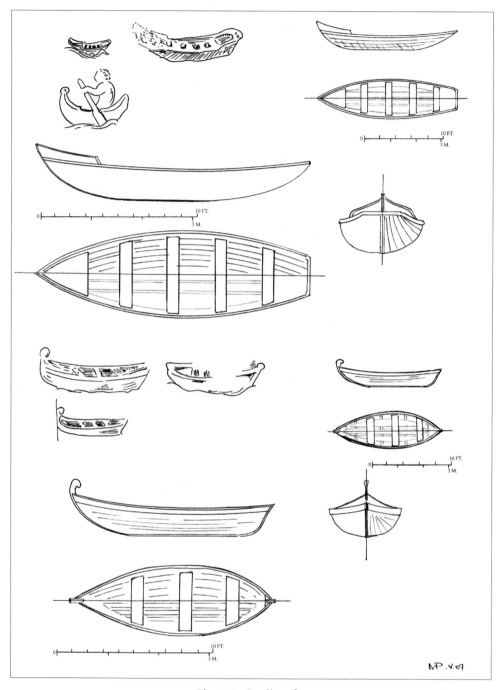

Plan 23. Small craft.

would be appropriate. Scene XXXIV[8] of Trajan's Column shows such a ship being rowed and also what looks like an awning above the centre deck, as well as the prominent bracket for securing the side rudder.

Although on the small side, these barges could be used in smaller tributaries of the main rivers and through locks; needing only small crews yet bearing a useful load. Their obvious employment in large numbers also ensured that enough could be concentrated to enable the Danube to be bridged, for example. It is probable that a large gangplank would be included in the ship's inventory to enable stores to be conveyed to a riverbank and even that spars or booms and tackle were included so that a loading or unloading derrick could be rigged. What appear to be prominent rivets are shown on the aft cabin sides, indicating perhaps that they were of overlapping planks, secured clinker-fashion. Dimensions: length overall: 48 feet (14.63m); waterline: 42 feet (12.8m); beam overall and waterline (max.): 16 feet (4.87m); draft 3 feet (914mm); freeboard (to bulwark): 5 feet 9 inches (1.75m).

SMALL CRAFT

Colour Plate XIV (Plan 23)
Upper drawing: a smallish scow, 17 feet (5.33m) × 5 feet (1.52m) beam.

After sketches from (top left) a relief from Portus, *c.* AD 200; (lower left) third-century AD relief from Ostia; (right) late second-century AD relief, also from Portus.

Lower drawing: small ship's boat or tender, 13 feet overall (3.96m) × 4.5 feet (1.37m) beam.

After sketches from (top) third-century AD mosaic; (lower left) the same; (right) a relief now in the Torlonia Museum, Rome.

NOTES

1 Haywood, *Dark Age Naval Power.*
2 Austin and Rankov, *Exploratio.*
3 The roman numerals refer to the photographic catalogue of the German Archaeological Institute, Rome. Full-size casts of the panels can be seen at the Museo della Civilta Romana, Rome.
4 A similar interpretation was reached in Bounegru and Zahariade, *Les Forces Navales du Bas Danube et de la Mer Noire.* However, their suggested dimensions for the two do not differentiate sufficiently between them. If the dimensions of the 'river' version suggested here are reasonable (see below), the dimensions for the sea-going version would, it is suggested, need to be greater.
5 German Archaeological Institute catalogue numbers.
6 Vegetius, IV.33.
7 Livy, XXIX.25.
8 German Archaeological Institute catalogue numbers.

THE LATER EMPIRE: FOURTH AND FIFTH CENTURIES AD

After the upheavals of the late third century AD, the old Imperial fleets of the early empire had been reduced to a shadow of their former splendour. Diocletian (AD 285–305) reorganised the remainder into ten squadrons dispersed along the Rhine and Danube frontiers, together with an Italian fleet, a fleet for the eastern areas (the Black Sea and Aegean) and the 'British' fleet, the only one to have retained any semblance of its former identity and integrity. There is an almost total lack of iconography for this period and little in the way of literary sources.

The traditional designs can be assumed to have continued in use at least to the 320s, when new warship concepts started to be introduced. This is evident from the accounts of the civil war Battle of the Hellespont in AD 323 between the fleets of Licinius and Constantine. Licinius' fleet was said to be of 350 triremes,[1] although another source gives the more reasonable figure of 200 triremes, all drawn from eastern fleets and presumably of established design. They were to be defeated, however, by Constantine's fleet of 200 or, in the more reasonable account, 80 'triaconters'.[2] This is, to say the least, an odd, almost eccentric description, bearing in mind the antiquity of the term for a type of ship that had not been seen in centuries and which, had it been resurrected, would have been easy prey for the triremes. Assuming that the term has been accurately translated and passed down to us, then it was clearly used to indicate a totally new type, presumably powered by thirty oars and certainly capable of defeating triremes and to do this so thoroughly that the trireme disappears from history completely. No one thought of building any more, and the link with the ancient types of ship and their rowing systems was thus broken. The new ships bore no similarity to the earlier Mediterranean warships and regrettably there does not survive any other indication of the details of Constantine's ships. It is worth noting that the location of the battle probably played a significant part. On the face of it a trireme with over a hundred oars would have had a huge advantage over any ship powered by only thirty. The battle, however, took place in the narrow confines of the Dardanelles, where the trireme's advantage of speed and manoeuvrability were severely limited. The battle still leaves the question, what was it that made Constantine's ships so superior?[3]

On the river frontiers, the open boat types (see Chapter 6) continued in widespread use on the Rhine and Danube and their tributaries. It is during the fourth century AD that the name '*lusoria*' emerges for them. The fourth century AD saw a return to a more aggressive, forward defence of the river frontiers, with counter-attack and raiding into the barbarian sides of the rivers and their tributaries. These types were ideally suited to this very fluid form of small-action warfare.

For the northern seas, earlier designs evolved from their Mediterranean ancestry and gradually changed to a more local style to suit their operating environment. They also changed, at least in part, to the increasing use of the plank-on-frame building method as it replaced the shell-first method. The ships were, however, still capable of overawing any barbarian craft foolish enough to venture against them. Another factor which should not be overlooked was an increasing shortage of available manpower at a time of continually increasing enemy seaborne activity. The changes can be seen by comparing the ship of Hadrian (AD 117–38)[4] on the coin commemorating some of the Emperor's travels (Fig. 81) and which is obviously similar to those of Trajan examined in the last chapter (which in turn emanate from earlier designs) with the ship on another coin (Fig. 82) from southern Turkey of the mid- to late third century AD. Finally, by the late fourth century AD, the line of development of ancient ships had stopped, the new types that replaced them bearing not even a superficial resemblance.

The last foray of the western fleet of the Roman Navy was as part of the joint east and west fleet which sought to recover the province of Africa (northern Tunisia), but was poorly commanded and destroyed by the Vandals near Carthage in AD 467.[5] These fleets seem to have used ships of a type which later would evolve into the famous *dromon* of the the eastern Roman fleet, which continued and became what is now referred to as the Byzantine Navy.

RHINE PATROL SHIP

Colour Plate XX (Plan 24)
This example of a warship, presumably on the River Moselle, is fashioned after a stone monument from Neumagen in Germany of *c.* AD 300 (Fig. 83).[6] The ship seems to have a deck cargo of large barrels and a number of men, of the usual exaggerated size, are shown on deck. A helmsman is depicted in the stern ahead of a small cuddy, with another man in the bow, apparently addressing the rest of the men, who are facing forward. It is remotely possible that they are meant to represent the rowers, rowing while standing and facing forward in the Mediterranean fashion, but this seems unlikely: firstly, only six men are shown for twenty-two oars; secondly, this would raise the centre of gravity and thus increase instability in the ship; thirdly, it would leave them very vulnerable to archery and other missiles in the confines of river operations. Finally, it is not very efficient. As the ship has a substantial deck cargo, it can be assumed to have a deck and to be similarly substantial itself. As this ship bears a strong resemblance to the seagoing types next discussed (and seen in Fig. 82) it may be that it is in fact meant to

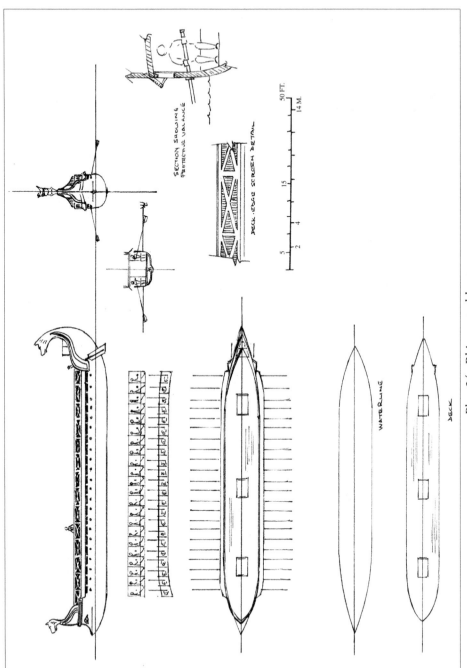

Plan 24. Rhine patrol boat.

Figure 81. Gold aureus of Hadrian, found in England, which could thus show a ship of the northern fleets, in use to transport the Emperor.

Figure 82. Bronze coin from southern Turkey, mid- to late third century AD, showing a different form of warship.

Figure 83. Rhine patrol ship. From a mortuary statue of *c.* AD 250–300, from Neumagen, Germany, showing such a ship with a deck cargo of large barrels.

represent a seagoing ship. However, the monument was found at Neumagen, only a few miles downstream from Trier (Augusta Treverorum, a major Roman base). This in itself is hardly conclusive, but could suggest a river ship, continuing the two-tier approach to river warships posited in Chapter 6.

From this assumption, the general character of the ship would therefore suggest more than a smallish open boat and is thus interpreted as a fully decked monoreme ship, traditional in overall concept and powered by a reme of twenty-two oars per side. Bow and stern are both closed and stem and sternposts are surmounted by figureheads of wolves or mastiffs. This form of ship also appears on coins and mosaics of similar date (see below), suggesting an overall fashion in the look of warships for use in northern waters. The animal heads surmounting the stem and sternposts could even hark back to an earlier, Celtic tradition. Coins of *c.* 100 BC from northern Gaul show ships with these features.[7]

There is a pierced bulwark along the deck edge and below this appears a flange or valance, angled outboard and from beneath which the oars emerge, no other oar-ports being shown. The valance is interpreted as a protective screen to shelter a line of open ports serving as a ventilation course for the lower deck and its occupants. No rig is shown. The steering oar appears to be retracted and would have little effect upon a ship forging upstream against a strong current, where the oars could easily suffice to keep it on course. As the port steering oar is shown, another is assumed for the starboard side.

The height of the hull between the oarports and the waterline is exaggerated and the ship hull foreshortened to fit the stone. The installation of twenty-two oars per side seems not unreasonable (see Fig. 9 for a precedent) and has been retained, in turn dictating the length of the ship. Similarly, a reasonably short oar is desirable to operate in restricted riverine conditions and being able to operate it at a reasonable angle also dictates a lower height of hull above the waterline than that shown by the sculpture. Any lack of visibility astern arising from the closed-in form of the stern does not seem to have been a problem, and the reasonably simple format of the ship has been suited to short-duration patrolling of the Rhine river system.

The ram is a small, upturned point. The anticipated enemy vessels were not the heavily armoured galleys of yore, but smaller, lighter, probably open boats, for which this form would have been deadly enough. No sailing rig is indicated on the original.
Suggested crew: 2 officers, 44 rowers, 4 archers, 12 marines, 3 sailors; total: 65.
Dimensions: length overall: 92 feet (28m); waterline: 86 feet (26m); beam overall: 12 feet (3.66m); waterline: 10 feet (3.05m); draft: 3 feet 6 inches (1.07m); freeboard: 18 inches (457mm).

WARSHIPS OF THE 'CLASSIS BRITANNICA'

The few representations from the north in this period seem fairly uniform in overall concept, which seems, superficially at least, to be monoreme ships with high stem and sternposts, mostly matching and in the fashion of the Rhine patrol ship, i.e. with animal-head finials (a continuation of the Celtic tradition, an inspiration, perhaps, for the later 'dragon ships' of the Vikings). Unfortunately they are also small (on coins) or simplified (mosaic). In all of them, oars emerge from hull-side ports, beneath cross-balustraded side screens with more solid bow and stern sections. The ships appear to be fully decked, some with a cuddy or shelter built into the stern. Most, but not all, are shown with a mast rigged with fore and back stays, sometimes doubled. This may not have been a permanent fixture, and the rig could be dropped when not needed (see Fig. 82). The artemon or foremast is now entirely absent.

The ships doubtless evolved to suit the northern waters and were beamier, of more substantial build, with higher freeboard and sides to make them more weatherly and

Figure 84. Warship of the *Classis Britannica* on a coin of Allectus. The ship is stylised, with a spur-like ram and high stem and sternposts. It appears to be a monoreme with a nominal four oars and a side rudder indicated. There is a decorated bulwark above the oars, with the heads of the men above that. A mast with fore and back stays can be discerned, together with a top but no yard (author's collection).

Figure 85. Commemorative medallion of Constantius, issued upon the restoration of Britannia to the Empire and the ending of the secession of Carausius and Allectus in September AD 296. The ship is similar to the Rhine ship but a seagoing version, proved by the fact that Constantius used the *Classis Britannica* for the campaign and then cruised to Scotland and the Orkneys with the fleet. (Photograph © the author, image reproduction for non-commercial purposes courtesy of the Trustees of the British Museum.)

perhaps with flatter bottoms, all following the Celtic tradition going back to the ships described by Caesar.[8] As with the case of the riverine and seagoing versions of the liburnians in Chapter 7, it has been assumed that, in view of their overall general similarity in appearance, there were riverine (as described earlier) and seagoing versions of these ships. The evidence of their appearance and use in a seagoing context is in the coin of the usurper Allectus (AD 293–6), commander of the British fleet (Fig. 84) and a commemorative medallion of the Emperor Constantius, who defeated him (Fig. 85). There is also a fourth-century AD mosaic from Somerset (Fig. 86), and in all of these cases, the ships are in use at sea, which requires a more substantial ship than the river patrol craft.

On the coin of Allectus, the heads of the men appear over the rail and they could thus be rowing. The medallion is similar to the coin, except that eight oars but only four heads are shown, and on the mosaic the heads are even more obviously not those of rowers, who, as with Trajan's ships, can be assumed to be shielded by the side screens. In all of these cases, the ships are shown with matching bow and stern posts surmounted by some device, that of the stern being slightly the higher.

Figure 86. Sketch of part of a third-century AD mosaic from Somerset, with a ship very similar in concept to the previous examples.

To translate this evidence into a realistic form, let us first consider the ships in their operational environment. The ships of Rome's enemies, from examples found at Bruges, Belgium, dating from *c.* AD 200 and Nydam, Denmark, of *c.* AD 300, together with various pictorial representations,[9] were open, double-ended, clinker-built monoremes, similar in overall concept and which evolved into the later Sutton Hoo (*c.* AD 600) and Viking ships. None is equipped with the ram. Against these ships the Romans can be assumed to have deployed their technological superiority and to have employed the additional power of a larger warship, perhaps a bireme, to make more effective the ram with which they are shown to have been equipped. As to the form of the ram itself, the iconography seems to show a simple, pointed spur, almost a return to the original form (Fig. 21). Recalling the tendency this had to stick or become fouled in an enemy hull and the consequent development of the square-in-section forms which persevered thereafter, it is suggested (and in the absence of better evidence it can be no more than a suggestion) that these pointed rams were also square in section. Finally, the rams do not project as far ahead of the hulls as formerly.

Although the evidence seems to show only a notional single reme of a few oars, bearing in mind the difficulties of interpretation from such few and small examples and the constraints of the media used, it would not mean that all of the ships were the same. Once again, therefore, a two-tier approach is posited, with large bireme warships, easily capable of destroying any opposing barbarian ships, supported by smaller, monoreme ships. This accords with definitions given by Vegetius, writing in the late fourth or early fifth century AD. [10]

Estimates of the dimensions for the bireme ship could be based either on the seagoing liburnian in Chapter 6, or on a quadrireme.[11] With the increasing shortage of manpower in the late Empire in mind, the less demanding liburnian has been preferred, using as a starting point the seagoing example from Chapter 7, with the same rowing system. To adapt it for use in northern waters, the freeboard has been increased to 3 feet (915mm), and to retain the same operating angles (26 and 15 degrees) the oars have been lengthened to 18 feet (5.5m), increasing the gearing to four, at the upper limit of acceptability. To alleviate this and give more room for the rowers, the interscalmium is increased to 3 feet 6 inches (1.04m) and the hull cross-section enlarged to increase displacement and to counter the added top-weight. The crew was retained at 86 (3 officers, 6 sailors, 15 marines and 62 rowers). The break in the forward bulwark for a boarding gangway does not appear in any of these ships, so presumably boarding was not the preferred method for dealing with the types of craft against which they were pitted. Ramming would have been effective and with their opponents lacking any form of artillery, there was no need for all-covering armour protection, hence the open side screens. The greater height of these ships made boarding by their enemies very difficult, to say the least. Further, although the Rhine craft is decked for the reasons given, to add a top deck with a bulwark above it for the deck crew makes this ship look top-heavy and out of proportion and causes the interpretation to cease to resemble the evidence and thus fail.

The result (Fig. 87) was unsatisfactory. Although it more or less accords with the iconography, there is no upper deck to accommodate the figures that are shown, and if there is to be such a deck, no bulwark around it is shown as distinct from a ventilation course, only a single line of balustrading being indicated. Further, the ship is still a liburnian in effect, which as a type was always intended to fulfil a light, supporting role, subsidiary to the main combat units of the fleet. Despite the fact that the class had evolved and grown, it was never the principal combat element, nor was it intended to be. Against even the larger barbarian craft (the Nydam boat was 79 feet/24m in length), it does not give the overwhelming capability needed and of which the Roman designers were certainly capable.

The representations are, of course, foreshortened as to length and logically, also presumably as to height. The apparent omission of discernable separate ventilation and upper-deck levels need not influence the interpretation, any more than the acceptance that there were more than four or eight oars per side, or that they could have been biremes. A further consideration is whether at that time and in this theatre of operations such major warships could still be built. This led to a reconsideration of the remains of the only relevant Roman seagoing hull that has to date been found in Britain and which dates from the period now under consideration, namely the 'County Hall ship'.[12] This was a 38 foot (11.6m) section of hull of a Roman ship dated to AD 285, built on the south coast of England, using the full Mediterranean mortice-and-tenon system, rather than by the local plank-on-frame method. It was estimated to be a merchant hull 60–70 feet (18.3–21.3m) in length with a beam of about 15 feet (4.6m), but extrapolation of the surviving lines suggests that the complete hull could have been anything between 70 feet (21.3m) and 130 feet (39.6m) and the beam up to 18.5 feet (5.6m). Such an interpretation would offer a length-to-beam ratio of from 4:1 at the shorter length, the proportions of a merchantman, to 7:1 when extended, just right for a warship.[13] It has already been seen how the strong hull emanating from the 'Mediterranean method' was evolved and strengthened to withstand the shock of ramming attacks and that none of

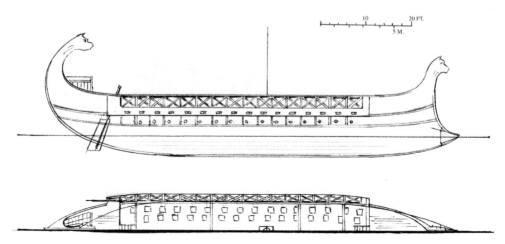

Figure 87. Adaptation of the seagoing liburnian from Chapter 7 to suit the perceived characteristics for a ship of the *Classis Britannica*.

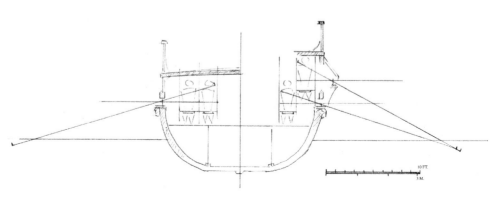

Figure 88. Rowing systems for the amended design, as a double-banked monoreme and as a bireme. The section is approximately that of the 'County Hall ship', with original stanchion and thwart positions; freeboard 3 feet 6 inches (1070mm).

the ships built by the other method appear to have had rams. The hull is, however, flat-bottomed and of shallow keel in the manner of merchant ships and in the absence of any indication, such as an oar-port, of a rowing system, cannot be confirmed as a warship. Nevertheless, the point is made that hulls of suitable construction and size were possible at that time and place. Applying all of this to recast the design, it was lengthened to 130 feet (39.6m), with the number of rowers increased to twenty-seven per side in the upper reme and twenty-six per side in the lower, enclosed within a fully decked-over hull, to produce a far better-proportioned ship.

This redesign (Plan 25) provides a better fighting platform for the larger number of marines that can now be carried, perhaps even with some artillery. It also offers a rowing compartment in which the oarsmen have a large degree of protection from the elements, helping them to maintain better condition for longer than their opponents, who were in boats totally open to the sea and weather. Finally, the larger ship, as well as offering the required superiority, retains the overall proportions of the iconography. The size now reached is approximately that of a trireme, and the deck height above the water (at 9½ feet/2.9m) virtually that of a quinquireme. However, the length would provide the speed and power required, and the height is a corollary of the need for increased freeboard. Further, all of this additional bulk and top-hamper would be better served by the greater displacement provided by the more full-bottomed cross-section and form of the 'County Hall ship'. A further exercise (the lower elevation, Plan 25)), envisaged the ship as a monoreme with 23 foot (7m) oars, double banked and operated at a mean angle of 15 degrees, geared at 2.8. This reduced the deck height by 2 feet (610mm) and offered a satisfactory alternative arrangement, but also reduced the essential motive power by the equivalent of fourteen manpower (Fig. 88; see also the section on the *sexteres* in Chapter 5), a penalty for which the smallish reduction in height was possibly not sufficient justification. Elevations of both versions are included (Plan 25).

Suggested crew: 4 officers, 6 sailors, 30 marines, 106 rowers; total: 146.

Dimensions: length overall: 130 feet (39.6m); waterline: 123 feet (37.5m); beam overall: 18 feet (5.5m); waterline: 14 feet 6 inches (4.42m); draft: 4 feet 6 inches (1.37m); freeboard: 3 feet (915mm).

For the complementary scout ships, Vegetius confirms that 'to the larger ships are attached scouting skiffs [*scaphae exploratoriae*] having about twenty oarsmen on each side, these the Britons call *picati*. They are used on occasion to perform descents or to intercept convoys of enemy shipping or by studious surveillance to detect their approach or intentions.'[14] He goes on to relate how the ships, their sails, rigging and even the uniforms of their crews, were camouflaged by being painted and coloured blue 'so as to lie hidden with greater ease when scouting by day or by night'. Vegetius is clearly referring in this chapter to seagoing craft alone as he deliberately and specifically mentions river craft separately at the end of his Book IV, Chapter 46.

In the absence of any representation that can be positively identified as being of this type, there is only the indication that it was powered by 'about twenty oarsmen on each side' and of the overall style of ships of this period to assist in realising a reconstruction. Accordingly, the interpretation of the ship (Plan 26) must be purely conjectural

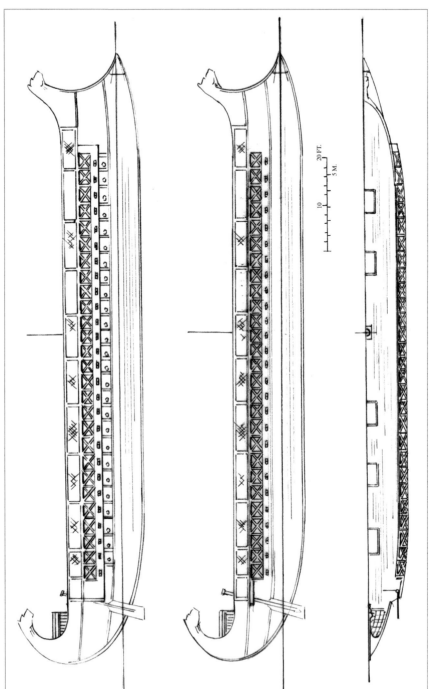

Plan 25. Warships of the *Classis Britannica*.

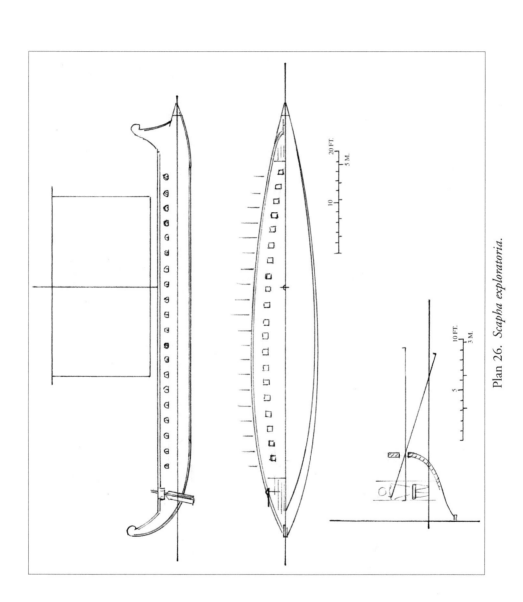

20 FT.

5 M.

10

10 FT.

3 M.

5

Plan 26. *Scapha exploratoria.*

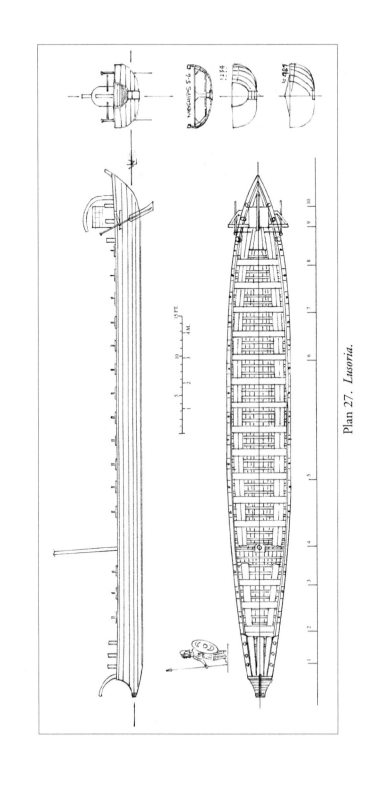

Plan 27. *Lusoria.*

and is drawn as a monoreme of forty oars, yielding a length of between 80 and 90 feet (24.4–27.4m), with sides built up above the oar-ports to afford some protection to the rowers and carrying the by now ubiquitous single mast rig. The ship is open, with no covering top deck and with the built-up sides, has no need of the open-work side screens of the previous type, appearing more like the example in Figure 82. As the ship is intended for scouting and low-level combat, a nominal number of marines is carried. The interscalmium is 3 feet (915mm), with an oar of 15 feet (4.5m), gearing of 3.75 and operated at 17 degrees.

Suggested crew: 2 officers, 6 marines, 4 sailors and 20 rowers; total: 32.

Dimensions: length overall: 86 feet (26.2m); waterline: 81 feet (24.7m); beam overall: 13 feet 6 inches (4.1m); waterline: 12 feet (3.7m); draft: 3 feet (915mm); freeboard: 2 feet (610mm).

RIVER CRAFT, A 'LUSORIA'

Colour Plate XXI (Plan 27)

The development and deployment of specialised river warships discussed in Chapter 6 continued, as evidenced by the discovery of five wrecks of fourth-century AD river warships at Mainz on the Rhine.[15] In their overall concept and form these boats are very similar to the earlier Danube boats.

The ships are lightly built, plank-on-frame and carvel. There are no mortice and tenon joints between the hull strakes. The hulls seem to have been built inverted over a moulding frame, with permanent frames added once the shell was removed from the mould. The boats were mostly made from oak, with iron fixings and caulked with pitch.

As with the earlier Danube boats, there is no separate rowing crew. In these ships all crew are combatants, harking back to the earliest days of naval warfare.

In these ships also can be seen the development of the more aggressive policies of the fourth century AD. As well as for the more mundane patrols and duties, they are clearly intended for use in more shallow river reaches and up tributaries for raids and interdiction into barbarian lands, making optimum use of the manpower aboard. It is assumed that the blunt ram-like projection was tipped with bronze and was more than sufficient in the unlikely event of finding an enemy to ram. In any event it would help to protect the bow timbers when pulling the boat onto a river bank. The small open area in the bow is to allow troops to get ashore quickly on touching the river bank and also as a platform for archers.

A light sailing rig is assumed, with an open section forward of the mast to allow stowage of sails and rig. Both forward and right aft there are suggestions of vertical bars, which could be used to mount shields or protective screens. A small cuddy at the stern, perhaps a wicker frame covered with leather, protects the helmsman, who is provided with twin steering oars.

The wrecks discovered fall into two types, the *lusoria*,[16] which is a pure warship, and another, shorter and beamier, which would appear to be a transport type. Perhaps this

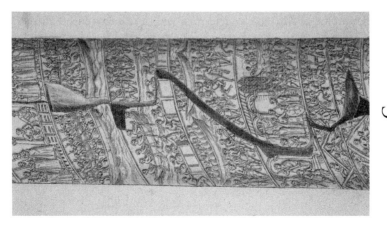

Figure 89. Three drawings of sections of the fifth-century AD Column of Arcadius, formerly in Constantinople, showing troops of the East Roman forces being transported in a standardised type of transport ship, together with a few smaller boats. (Courtesy of the Master and Fellows of Trinity College, Cambridge.)

latter was a *caudicaria* (or *iudicaria* on the Danube). It is estimated that the type could cruise at 7 knots under oars, with a 10-knot dash speed (ignoring the effect of the river current). Clearly successful and doubtless with several variants, it remained in service for a long time, being on the Danube in AD 412[17] and still mentioned under Justinian (AD 527–65).

Suggested crew: 2 officers; 3 sailors; 4 archers; 40 rowers/marines; total: 49.

Dimensions: Length overall: 66 ft. (21.77m); waterline: 63 feet 6 inches (19.4m); beam overall: 8 feet (2.4m); waterline: 7 feet (2.1m); draft: 1 foot (305mm); freeboard: 2 feet (610mm).

Oars: 30 at 10 feet (3m).

MILITARY TRANSPORT, FIFTH CENTURY AD

Colour Plate XXII (Plan 28)

The inspiration for the envisioning of such a type is the pictures of ships of the East Roman forces in about AD 400, a set of three sixteenth-century drawing of the Column of Arcadius (Emperor in the East AD 395–408) in Constantinople, destroyed by an earthquake in 1715 (Fig. 89). The drawings are very detailed and of a very high standard and one can only hope that they are entirely accurate, especially as they are all that survives. The ships generally seem to be fairly uniform in size, rig and format and it is reasonably safe to take them as accurate representations of a contemporary type rather than an artistic convention or a stylised form. For the most part, the ships of this standard type bear no relationship to previous Roman ship types, being double-ended, without rams and most have a protruding 'beak' atop the stem. In the absence of any obvious function, this 'beak' can be considered only as a fashion of the period.[18] They have a single mast stepped amidships, supported by stays and shrouds, the latter showing ratlines. Not all of the ships display the full standing rigging, and any yards seem to have been lost in the narrow spiral banding of the column. Presumably most of the ships shown under way are being powered by the (hidden) sailing rigs, but a couple can be seen being rowed by a single reme, across the open bulwark.

No steering oars or side rudders can be discerned, but two of the ships in Figure 89A and three in Figure 89B have indications which could well show stern-hung rudders (see also the section on rudders in Chapter 3). In another, slightly later (*c.* AD 600) mosaic from Ravenna (Fig. 90) ships in a harbour are shown with conventional side rudders.

All are being used as troop transports (with the size of the figures exaggerated in relation to that of the ships, as always) and are, in the absence of rams and other attributes of ancient warships, interpreted as a standard type of seagoing military transport.

As to size, I have guessed, arbitrarily but hopefully not unreasonably, at 90 feet (27.4m) in length, with a length-to-beam ratio of 6:1, giving a beam of about 16 feet (4.9m), relatively fine but suitable for a fast transport, with a draft of about 4 feet 6 inches (1.37m) on a well-rounded hull, so configured for cargo and decked overall. The

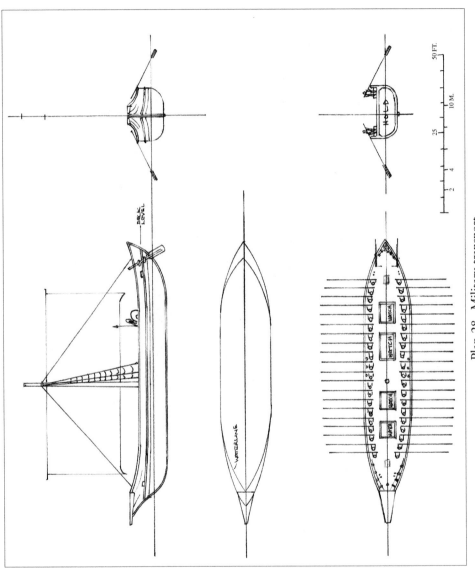

Plan 28. Military transport.

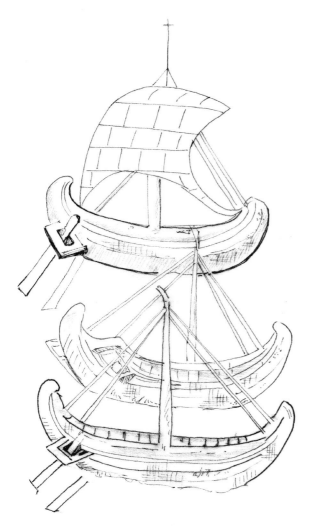

Figure 90. Detail from a sixth-century AD mosaic, still in the church of S. Apollinare Nuovo, Ravenna, of three merchant ships. Although crude and with several anomalies in depiction, it does clearly show twin steering oars and permanently stepped masts with twin fore and back stays (after Bass).

length would allow about 60 feet (18.3m) on each beam for auxiliary rowers, enough for 20 per side, given an interscalmium of 3 feet (915mm) and assuming one man per oar of 17 feet (5.18m). Although the sailing rig is considered to be the principal method of propulsion, benches have been included on the model and four big hatches included for cargo handling.

Dimensions: length overall: 90 feet (27.4m); waterline: 76 feet (23.2m); beam overall: 16 feet (4.9m); waterline: the same; draft: 4 feet 6 inches (1.37m); freeboard, to bulwark: 5 feet (1.53m).

Oars: 40 at 17 feet (5.18m), gearing 3.4.

Figure 91. Detail showing a warship, from a fifth-century AD manuscript of Virgil's *Aeneid*.

Figure 92. Detail from a fifth-century AD manuscript of the *Iliad*, showing ships moored with sails furled. The topsails are not otherwise attested and may be a result of subsequent variations (after Torr).

LATE ROMAN WARSHIP

Colour Plate XXIII (Plan 29)

These last of a long line of Roman warships represent once more a total break with the past, but do show connections with later types, having the appearance, in fact, of what can only be described as an 'embryo *dromon*'. There are only a couple of miniscule sketches from which to reconstruct these last ships. A warship from a fifth-century AD manuscript (Fig. 91) shows a ship with oars in a single reme and a traditional steering oar or side rudder, with bow and sternpost projections and a rising ram. Another illustration (Fig. 92) from a manuscript of similar date shows the sterns of warships at anchor, side rudders emerging from box structures in the bulwark. Interestingly, these ships are shown with topsail yards bearing furled topsails. Some further corroboration would be needed before attributing this innovation to the reconstruction of these ships.

They are interpreted to be fully decked, in confirmation of which, Procopius, describing warships of the North Africa expedition of AD 533, states that they are 'single-reme and having decks overhead to reduce to a minimum the chance of the rowers being hit by enemy missiles'.[19] He goes on to relate how such a ship was called a *dromon*, the first mention of the term and we can assume that this ship is the ancestor of that type. In Figure 91, troops are shown on deck and there are large oar 'windows' to allow ventilation for the oarsmen below and for the oars to be operated across an open hull side, as well as through an oar-port. A single mast is stepped, carrying a single rectangular sail. Only eight oars are shown on the side, presumably for the sake of simplicity, but the ship must have been of a reasonable size to give enough weight to justify the inclusion of a ram. There is nothing in Figure 92 to contradict this, as no detail of any rowing system is shown, although the general stern configuration and prominent steering oar-boxes are clearly seen.

Accordingly, if it is assumed that the ship is to be of 40 oars, a length of 110 feet (33.5m) overall is indicated. As a seagoing ship with a reasonable freeboard and a height dictated by the need for the upper deck to clear the rowers below, especially when the weight of the rig and men on deck is added, a beam of 16 feet (4.9m) and a draft of 4 feet (1.22m) should give stability. However, as all of these late representations show the rig mounted, perhaps it was permanently so and therefore a deeper keel could be considered, increasing the daft to perhaps as much as 5 feet 6 inches (1.7m).

It is suggested that the oars are longer and double-manned, which seems appropriate in a monoreme of such size, as are the twin steering oars. In the absence of standing rigging being shown, fore and back stays and shrouds are provided, as shown on the other contemporary, if differing, types of ship, with the mast permanently stepped.

Suggested crew with 40 2-man oars: 6 officers, 12 sailors, 30/40 marines, 80 rowers; total: 128/138.

Dimensions: length overall: 110 feet (33.5m); waterline: 91 feet (27.7m); beam overall: 16 feet (4.9m); waterline: 15 feet (4.6m); draft: 4 feet (1.22m) to 5 feet 6 inches (1.7m); freeboard: 2 feet (610mm).

Oars: 40 at 20 feet (6m), gearing 3.3.

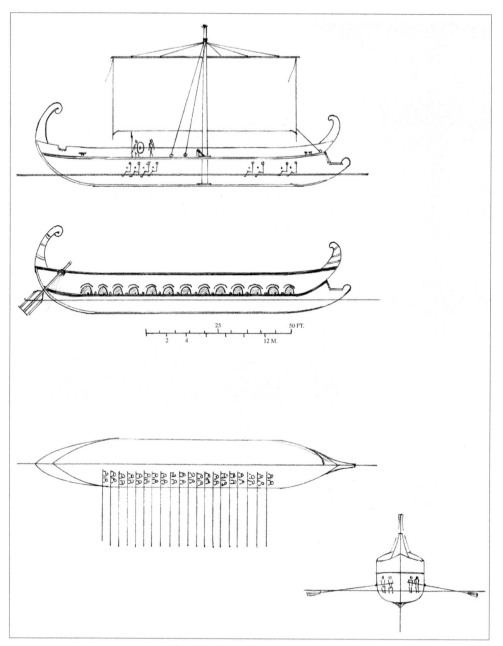

Plan 29. Late Roman warship.

NOTES

1 Zosimus, *Historia* II.22.
2 The sources agree on the nomenclature.
3 Pitassi, *The Navies of Rome.*
4 A gold aureus of the Emperor Hadrian, found in England, now in the British Museum.
5 Procopius, *The Vandalic Wars.*
6 Now in the Landesmuseum, Trier.
7 Ellmers, *Celtic Plank Ships 500 BC to AD 1000.*
8 Caesar, *The Battle for Gaul* III.13.
9 Haywood, *Dark Age Naval Power.*
10 Vegetius, IV.37.
11 Vegetius, IV.37 mentions 'ranks' of oarsmen, one for the smallest ships, the scouts, but also two, three, four and even five.
12 For a fuller consideration and a drawing of the recovered remains, see Marsden, 'Ships of the Roman Period and After', in Bass, *A History of Seafaring.*
13 See also the analysis in Grainge, *The Roman Invasions of Britain,* for another view.
14 Vegetius, IV.37.
15 These boats, together with reconstructions and models of them, are now housed in the Museum of Ancient Shipping at Mainz, Germany.
16 Vegetius, II.1 and IV.46.
17 Codex Theodosianus, VII.17.
18 For more recent examples of such fashions, note, for example, the bow shapes of US battleships of the 1920s and 1930s, or those of pre-World War II Japanese cruisers.
19 Procopius, *The Vandalic Wars* I.11.

9

TERMINUS

Over the course of the many centuries of Roman maritime endeavour, the several fleets that contributed to Rome's naval power had to grow, adapt and diversify. Starting with the operation of a few ships, either by acquiring them or copying them from the Etruscans and Greeks with whom they shared the peninsula, the Romans were propelled by the onset of the Punic Wars to themselves become a naval power and develop a major shipbuilding industry and to build first-rate major warships in large numbers.

The First Punic War (264–241 BC) was essentially a naval war in the waters around Sicily and the central Mediterranean; the course of the Second (218–202 BC) was, despite the brilliance of Hannibal, dictated by naval operations and strategy, stretching into the western and eastern parts of that sea.[1] It was the growth of these strategic considerations to encompass ever-increasing areas that then and later dictated the deployment in numbers of types of ship found to be best suited for the tasks in hand and to the progressive refinement of those types.

In the further expansion of Rome's empire, naval formations played a most important, in many cases crucial, role; for example, in the invasion of Britain. Expansion into Gaul (France) and then Britain brought a completely new operating environment for Roman shipping. For his operations in Gaul, Caesar initially brought ships from the Mediterranean and had others built locally, using Mediterranean designs and methods.[2] Although these ships proved reasonably adequate, their successors for the northern fleets were adapted to better suit local conditions, which were met by adapting and adopting some of the local maritime tradition and method, as indeed the Romans had done in other areas in the past. The result was that by the time of Hadrian (AD 117–38), the ships bore only a superficial resemblance to their ancestry (Fig. 81).

With the expansion to the riverine frontiers on the Rhine and Danube, yet another, operational environment imposed the need for more and different types of ship. Flotillas were in fact established on the Rhine probably by Caesar and on the Danube by Augustus in 15 BC. This gave rise to the river warships, which seem to have been perfected quite early, certainly by the mid-first century AD. The Oberstimm boats (Chapter 6) are the earliest examples so far discovered, but there is a notable similarity and continuity in concept between them and the fourth-century Mainz boats (Chapter 8).

A factor affecting the evolution of the different types to suit the different areas was that 'the navy' could not be a unified service. Once the Romans expanded beyond the seas adjacent to the Italian peninsula during and after the Punic Wars (when Roman fleets had experienced operations in all parts of the Mediterranean basin), such a concept became impossible in practice. From Pompeius' war against the pirates of 67 BC, Roman fleets were permanently stationed in the eastern Mediterranean. With Augustus and the start of the Imperial Navy (from 27 BC), two main Italian fleets were established, one at Misenum (Miseno) on the Bay of Naples, to cover the western Mediterranean and the other at Ravenna, to cover the Adriatic and the east. Other fleets were added at Alexandria (Egypt) (with a subsidiary squadron in what is now Algeria), Syria and the Levant, the Aegean and the southern Black Sea. The Rhine had its own fleet and the Danube had one for the upper half and another for the lower half, the latter of which had its area extended to cover the northern Black Sea. The final fleet was formed to cover the northern coasts of Gaul and Britain.[3] Although this organisation of ten great fleets was radically altered by Diocletian (AD 285–305) into thirteen smaller, regional formations, the result was still several formations, each for its own individual area. Geography, therefore, as much as military circumstance, dictated that the navy had to have these several fleets, each suited to the peculiarities of its own operating area.

Several types of ship remained in service for very long periods, for example the *sexteres* and quinqueremes adopted in the mid-third century BC for the First Punic War remained with the fleets well into the first century AD, some 300 years later. Liburnians and triremes formed elements of Roman naval formations for an incredible 600 years or so (Appendix I). Without the advent of revolutionary new forms of weapon or propulsion, warships were not rendered obsolete; there was no 'Dreadnought revolution' as in 1905. Thus a form of warship which had proved itself was refined, but remained a valid operational type, able to meet the demands placed upon it. New types were evolved for a specific purpose, for example the almost universal military transport seen in Chapter 7, but overall a remarkable continuity is seen, only broken at the very end of the period under consideration by a breakdown in the infrastructure and in the circumstances of the time, rather than by any failing in the ships themselves. This is, of course, proved by the continuing use of the river warship types on the Danube by the Eastern Roman Empire after the fall of the West.

Faint echoes of the usages of the Roman Navy and its ships, honed over the long centuries of their existence, still resonate today in the language still in use on boats and ships. Thus a light, small boat is still called a skiff (*scapha*) and the stern-most deck is still the poop (*puppis*). The names of Roman warships remain popular for much more recent ships, for example, among British ships alone, *Diana* (Daring class destroyer), *Mars* and *Hercules* (battleships), *Apollo* (minelayer), *Juno* and *Minerva* (Leander class frigates) and *Triton* (submarine). Just as Roman seafarers would have witnessed the carrying of cork floats for use as mooring marker buoys and as life preservers in a wreck or for a man overboard,[4] cork is a substance that was still used in lifejackets and floats well into the twentieth century. The admiralty-type anchor so commonplace today in many sizes also had its origins with the Romans (Fig. 32).

Of those thousands of ships, for just a few examples of which interpretations have been attempted in this book, save for the few found by rivers and a few artefacts, nothing survives. The legacy of their service in first obtaining, then maintaining naval hegemony over and around Europe and the other areas within their remit is still valid, as control of those seas has been a determining factor in most of the great wars that have wracked the continent since, not least the two World Wars of the last century.

The ships that we have been considering started out as sufficient to voyage, trade and if opportunity arose, raid on quite a small scale. From that beginning, sufficient numbers of adequate ships capable of decisively beating all opponents had to emerge. Having done that, they had to become ships capable of patrolling and controlling what they had won and the resulting vast increase in maritime trade and commerce was the prize they achieved, a prize not to be equalled until comparatively recently.

NOTES

1   Pitassi, *The Navies of Rome*.
2   Caesar, *The Battle for Gaul* III.14; see also Cassius Dio.
3   Starr, *The Roman Imperial Navy*; Pitassi, *The Navies of Rome*.
4   Casson, *Ships and Seafaring*, quoting Pliny and others.

APPENDIX I –SERVICE LIVES OF SHIP TYPES

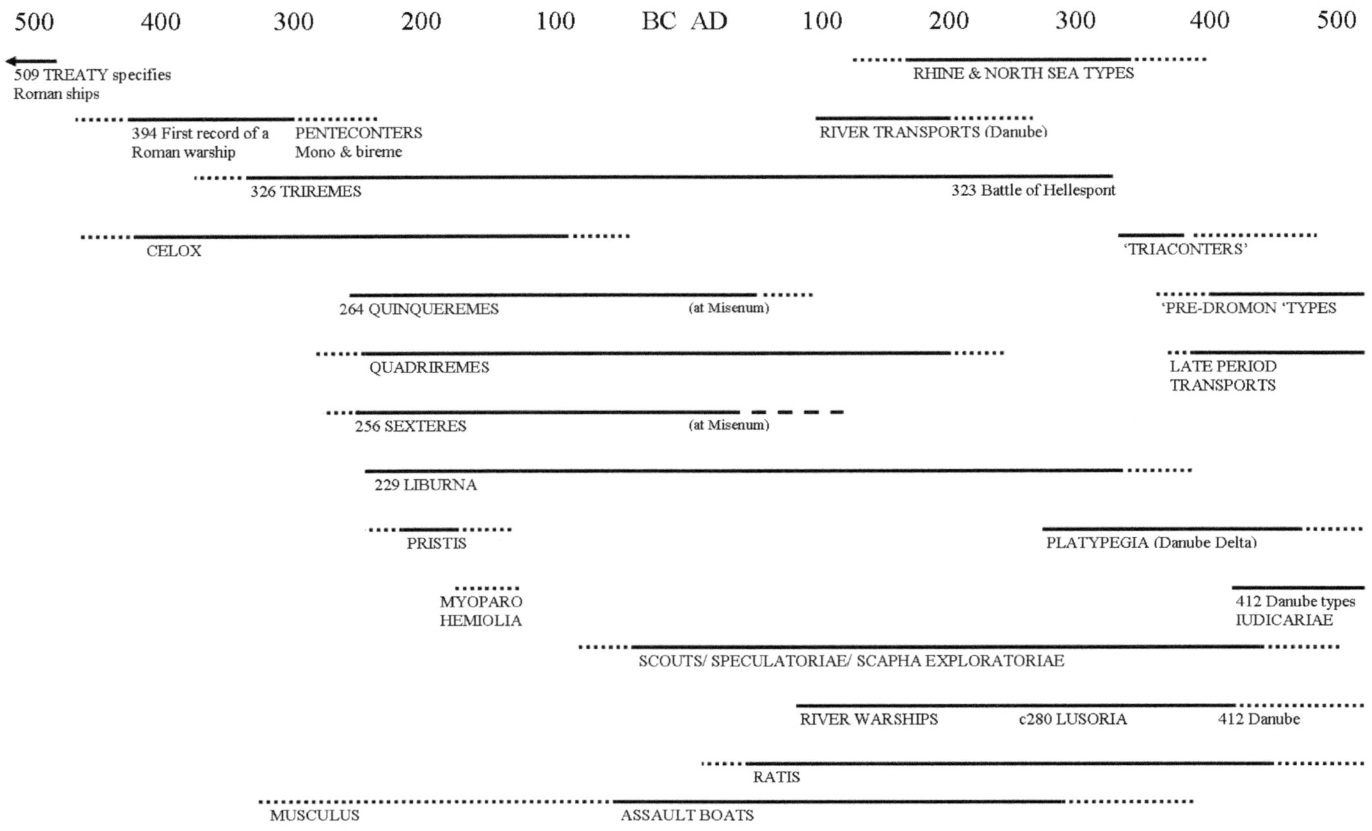
500
400
300
200
100
BC AD
100
200
300
400
500
509 TREATY specifies Roman ships
RHINE & NORTH SEA TYPES
394 First record of a Roman warship
PENTECONTERS Mono & bireme
RIVER TRANSPORTS (Danube)
326 TRIREMES
323 Battle of Hellespont
CELOX
'TRIACONTERS'
264 QUINQUEREMES
(at Misenum)
'PRE-DROMON 'TYPES
QUADRIREMES
LATE PERIOD TRANSPORTS
256 SEXTERES
(at Misenum)
229 LIBURNA
PRISTIS
PLATYPEGIA (Danube Delta)
MYOPARO HEMIOLIA
412 Danube types IUDICARIAE
SCOUTS/ SPECULATORIAE/ SCAPHA EXPLORATORIAE
RIVER WARSHIPS
c280 LUSORIA
412 Danube
RATIS
MUSCULUS
ASSAULT BOATS

Appendix II
Types of Roman Warship

AGRARIENSIS   type in use on Danube in AD 412. Possibly a reconnaissance/liaison type, of modest dimensions.

CAUDICARIA   generic term for a river lighter.

CELOX/CELOCES   first to fifth centuries BC. Small monoreme, two to twelve oars; used for dispatches or as senior officer's barge; perhaps tender to a big multi-reme; also small merchant galley.

'CONTER' TYPES   evolving from 'Homeric' types as monoremes, of tria (thirty) and penta (fifty) oars. Evolved further with bireme versions by the eighth century BC. The earliest types in Roman service, from 398 BC if not earlier. Roman classification of these types is not known. Continued in service in small numbers for ancillary uses until replaced by the *liburna* (q.v.) from *c.* 200 BC.

HEMIOLIA   Greek hybrid type especially favoured by pirates. A number pressed into Roman service in 149 BC as fast troop transports for Third Punic War, between Sicily and Africa. Not otherwise known in Roman service. See also *myoparo*.

IUDICARIA   type in use on the Danube in AD 412; could be synonymous with or local name for caudicaria (q.v.).

LIBURNA/LEMBUS   third century BC to *c.* late fourth century AD. Illyrian native craft of varying sizes, encountered in 229 BC. Many captured and used by Romans. Beamy monoreme, open, with no ram; the largest could carry up to circa fifty rowers plus twenty passengers and two horses. Developed by Romans as standard light warship, with variants of perhaps between thirty and sixty oars and used for liaison/reconnaissance/convoy escort/troop transport. Possibly separate seagoing and river versions by second century AD, of similar appearance but the former sturdier and with deeper draft. Variants known, L. Armata and L. Sagitta (in Black Sea), the former perhaps armoured and the latter with light artillery (Manuballistae?). Used by Emperor Julian on Danube in AD 361. Later became a generic name for a warship. See also *pristis*.

LUSORIA   from *c.* AD 280 to the sixth century AD. Originally a river pleasure craft. Used as a patrol/interdiction craft on Danube and Rhine in large numbers and in a variety of sizes. Successors to types of similar concept developed for river use in the late first century AD.

MUSCULUS   originally seems to have been a term for any small rowing boat, tender, dinghy, etc. Later a version developed as a small marine assault boat with recurved bow and raised poop for use on (at least) Danube and Rhone.

MYOPARO/MYOPARONES/PARONES/PARUNCULI   small open galley used for war/piracy; broader than normal for better seakeeping. Used once as a fleet tender by Romans (*c.* 125 BC) but not adopted as a type. Disappears after the 'Pirate War' of 67 BC. See also *hemiolia*: the two may be related or even the same vessel referred to by different names.

NAVIS FLUMINALIS   generic term for a river transport.

NAVIS FRUMENTARIUS   generic term for a supply ship.

NAVIS LONGA   generic term for a warship, as opposed to 'round ship' for a merchantman.

PLATYPEGIA   late third century AD. Special type for use in Danube Delta. Punt with raised prow and poop and stern cabin; light lateen sailing rig.

PRISTIS   third to second centuries BC. Similar to a *liburna* (q.v.); they were used together. Smallish ship with a ram. As early *liburnae* had no rams, *pristis* may have been a name for a version with one, to distinguish it. Also used as a convoy escort.

QUADRIERES/QUADRIREME   invented *c.* 399 BC, probably in Carthage or perhaps in Syracuse. Could have been in Roman service prior to the First Punic War, but certainly during and after it. Probably a bireme with each oar double-manned; economical and efficient, remained in service into the third century AD.

QUINQUEREMIS/QUINQUEREME   invented *c.* 399 BC at Syracuse. The 'five', probably a trireme arrangement with the top two remes double-manned. Became most common fleet battle type in First Punic War. Early Roman types heavy and slow to carry *corvus* and towers. Later refined and improved and was mainstay of Roman battle fleets to the first century BC. A few remained thereafter, but with no opponents, disappeared probably at end of first century AD.

RATIS/RATIARIA   first to fifth centuries AD. Rafts or pontoons used for temporary floating bridges on rivers; could have mast and sail; presumably made to a standard pattern.

SCAPHAE   generic term for a ship's boat.

SCAPHAE EXPLORATORIAE   first century BC onwards. Ship's boats, presumably of a more refined type and carried by larger warships specifically for scouting; akin to *pinnaces*. Monoreme with up to twenty oars per side. Could be camouflaged.

SEXTERES/HEXERES 'SIX'   introduced at Syracuse between 367 and 344 BC. Used in small numbers and as flagships by Carthaginians and Romans and one example at least was in the Misenum Fleet in the first century AD. Possibly a trireme with each oar double-manned, or a bireme with three men per oar.

SPECULATORIA/ SPECULATORIA NAVIS   from.first century BC. Class of smallish reconnaissance and dispatch vessels. This could be either the same as *liburnis exploratoriae* or a separate type. Alternatively it could be a name for the duty rather than a class of ship that is used for any ship engaged upon such a mission.

TECTA NAVIS   generic term for an armoured or even a full- decked and enclosed warship.

TESSARARIUS/TABELLARIA   dispatch boat. Probably used as a generic term for any ship so used, rather than for a specialised type.

TRIACONTERS (LATE)   AD 323 onwards. Appear at the Battle of Hellespont in Constantine's fleet. Presumably a new type.

TRIREMIS/TRIERIS/TRIREME   *c.* 326 BC to AD 323. Ram-equipped warship with three superimposed 'layers' or remes of rowers. Early examples in Roman service most likely followed Greek style; later they developed their own variants. Used in small numbers through the Punic War period, but became more numerous and widely used in Imperial fleets.

OTHER ROMAN TERMS FOR SHIPS AND BOATS

ACTUARIA   a merchant galley, thirty to fifty oars; *actuariola* (diminutive) a small *actuaria*, perhaps ten or so oars. Also used as a generic term for 'boat'.

BARIDES   a name for foreign ships or boats, particularly Egyptian.

CAMARAE   a type from the eastern Black Sea, first century AD; light build, twenty-five to thirty men, double-ended; could be rowed either way; flat bottom, low sides.

CORBITA   large merchant ships, first to second centuries BC.

CYBAEA   similar, used in Sicily, first century BC.

CYMBA   Phoenician merchant type or boat.

CAUPULUS   small boat.

GAUDEIA   a small craft, possibly North African type.

GESORETA   a small craft.

HIPPI   Phoenician merchant ship.

HORIA/HORIOLA   a small craft.

LENUNCULUS   small lighter or harbour boat.

LINTER   a small boat.

ONERARIA NAVIS   generic term for a merchantman.

ORARIA/ORIA/ORIOLE/ORARIA NAVIS   small coastal or river craft for traffic or fishing.

PHASELI   sailing passenger ferries, first centuries BC and AD.

PLACIDA   small boat.

PONTO/PONTONES   merchant type, possibly southern Gaul; also later, for pontoons.

PROSUMIA   a merchant type.

SCAPHA   generic term for a small boat or ship's tender.

STLATTA   a small river boat.

VECTORIA   passenger ferry, second century AD.

VEGEIIA   a small boat, possibly Gaulish.

VEHIGELORUM   a river craft.

VETUTIA   a small boat.

Appendix III
Gazetteer: Where to see Roman Boats and Ships

Aquileia, Italy   National Archaeological Museum. Bottom section of a ship hull, first to third centuries AD.

Ercolano/Herculaneum, Italy   On-site museum with small boats excavated from the former foreshore; first century AD.

Galilee, Israel   Local museum. Sea of Galilee fishing boat, first century AD.

Hastings, England   Shipwreck Heritage Centre. Some timbers of the second-century AD 'Blackfriars ship' and of the late third-century AD 'County Hall ship', both originally found in London.

Kyrenia, Cyprus   'The Kyrenia Wreck', small merchant ship, third century AD.

Mainz, Germany   The Museum of Ancient Shipping. Remains of five river warships with reconstructions and models; also two more from the Danube.

Marsala, Sicily   Marsala Regional Archaeological Museum. Part of the hull of a Carthaginian warship from the mid-third century BC (First Punic War period).

Marseilles, France   Musée Barely. Section of hull, second to third centuries AD.

Olbia, Sardinia   Twelve merchant hulls of fifth century AD and a mast of first century AD.

Ostia, Italy   Ancient Ships Museum. Remains of five boats and ships, second to fifth centuries AD.

Nea Faliro, nr Athens, Greece   The *Olympias*; not Roman but a modern reconstruction of a classical Athenian trireme.

Pisa, Italy   Museum of Ancient Ships and archaeological site. Current excavations of nine boats and ships, of sixteen or more discovered so far. Sixth century BC to fifth century AD.

Ravenna, Italy   Comacchio Museum, near Ravenna. Part of a merchant hull, late first century BC.

Split, Croatia   The Archaeological Museum. Very small section of a ship hull of indeterminate type and date.

Appendix IV
Glossary of Nautical Terms Used

ABOARD   that which is on, or in, or to go onto a ship.

ADMIRALTY ANCHOR   a type of metal anchor with a metal shaft, crossbar at the top and curved bottom bar with integral flukes.

AFT   relating to the rear portion of a ship.

AMIDSHIPS   relating to the middle portion of a ship's length.

ARTEMON   foremast and/or foresail of an ancient ship.

ASKOMATA   a usually leather 'sock' attached to the ship's side and tied around an oar shaft to prevent ingress of water through an oar-port.

ASTERN   a ship going backwards or relating to the rear part of a ship.

ATHWARTSHIPS   something across a ship from side to side.

AWNINGS   fabric screens deployed to give shelter from sun or weather.

BACK STAY   a rope or line helping to hold the mast upright, secured between the upper part of the mast to the rear deck.

BANKING   as in 'double-banking', multiplying the number of rowers plying one oar.

BARGE   a broad, flat-bottomed cargo carrier of medium size.

BEAK   alternative term for a ram.

BEAM   the width of a ship from side to side.

BENT (TO A YARD)   the attachment of a sail to a yard.

BITT   a fixed, vertical timber baulk to which ropes can be made fast, usually for mooring.

BOARDING BRIDGE   a device for bridging the space between engaged ships, to enable marines to cross.

BOLLARDS   smaller bitts (q.v.) to which ropes may be secured.

BOOM   a spar or pole along the foot of a sail or used for holding something at length such as the foot of a sail.

BOTTOM BOARDS   boards fitted in the bottom of an open boat to serve as a floor.

BOW   the foremost part of a ship.

BOWSPRIT   a pole projecting beyond the bow to carry or secure rigging.

BRACES   ropes attached to and used to control the ends of a yard.

BRAILS/BUNTLINES   ropes leading from the deck over the top and down the front (or bunt) of a sail through rings and secured to the bottom edge; by pulling on them, the sail can be taken in or shortened.

BROADSIDE   relating to the side of a ship.

BULWARK   the sides of an open ship above its highest deck.

CARLING   a short timber fixed fore and aft between two hull timbers.

CARVEL   method of hull construction where planks are fitted edge to edge.

CATCH   the point at which an oar blade enters the water at the beginning of the stroke.

CATHEAD   timber projecting from the forward hull for slinging anchors or aft for securing side rudders.

CAULKING   the forcing of material between the planks of a hull or deck to make them watertight.

CLEAT   a deck fitting or projection to which a rope can be made fast.

CLINCHER/CLINKER BUILT   method of hull construction where hull strakes are fixed together by being overlapped along their length.

COAMING   a lip or raised edge around an opening in a deck to prevent water from spilling over the edge.

CORVUS   a boarding bridge (q.v.) dropped onto an enemy deck and locked in place by a spike at the end.

CROW'S NEST   a platform near the top of a mast used as a lookout position.

CRUTCHES   temporary supports.

CUDDY   a small deck shelter.

DEADRISE   that part of the hull immediately above the keel before it widens to the full beam.

DECK   horizontal platform or floor in a ship.

DECK SHEER   the horizontal curve of a hull between the stem and stern.

DERRICK   a boom or pole rigged to act as a crane.

DISPLACEMENT   the amount of water moved aside or displaced by the immersion of a ship hull and providing a method for calculating the weight of the ship.

DOUBLE-ENDED   a ship whose hull tapers to a point at both bow and stern.

DRAFT   the depth of a ship in the water.

FASTENINGS   rivets, nails and other metal devices used in securing hull parts.

FLUKES (ANCHOR)   flattened vanes of an anchor to help it grip the sea bottom.

FLYING DECK   a deck erected above the hull proper.

FORECASTLE   the forward upper section of a hull and any structure upon it.

FOREDECK – the forwardmost upper deck of a ship.

FOREFOOT   the bottom of the stempost (q.v.) where it turns into the keel.

FOREMAST   the mast nearest to the bow of a ship.

FORESAIL   a sail rigged to the foremast or *artemon*.

FORESTAY   a rope or line helping to hold the mast upright, secured between the upper part of the mast to the forward deck.

FORWARD/FORRARD   relating to or towards the bow of a ship.

FRAMES/RIBS   strengthening constructions fitted within the hull and transversely to the length.

FREEBOARD   height between the sea surface and the lowest level of a ship's side or apertures such as oar-ports.

GANGWAY   plank(s) or structure used to enable access from ship to shore.

GARBOARD   the first plank of a hull, fitted either side of and immediately onto the keel.

GRAPNEL   a barbed hook attached to a line, thrown to ensnare a target.

HALLIARDS/LIFTS   lines between deck and masthead, used to hoist the yard or sails.

HARPAX/ HARPOON   type of grapnel (q.v.) shot from a catapult.

HATCHES   openings in a deck for access, ventilation or cargo handling.

HAWSER   extra-strong rope or cable for heavy loads.

HELMSMAN   the person who steers the ship.

HOGGING   when excessive stress is exerted upon the length of a hull by a high wave amidships, producing a tendency for the ends to sag under their own weight, straining the hull; the opposite of sagging.

HULL   the 'shell' of a ship, the main body of it which floats.

HYPOZOMATA   strong cords attached firmly between bow and stern, fixed at each end then tightened to pull them and thereby stiffen a hull longitudinally.

INBOARD   closer to the centre-line of a ship.

INTERSCALMIUM   the distance between tholes in the same reme.

JETTIED   something built out beyond the main body of a hull. See also sponson.

KEEL   the central spine of a hull from which the rest of the hull is built up.

KNEES   a 'knee'-shaped piece of wood used to reinforce the junction between perpendicular timbers.

LATEEN   corruption of 'Latin'. Type of sail and rig appearing in the late Empire.

LEE BOARDS   weather boards erected along a ship side to raise the bulwark height.

LENGTH-TO-BEAM RATIO   the figure produced by dividing the beam into the length.

MAINMAST   the principal mast of a ship; normally the second back from the bow.

MAINSAIL   the lowest sail on the mainmast, usually the largest on the ship.

MOORING   to fix a ship in a chosen position with ropes or anchors.

MORTICE AND TENON   a method of joining two pieces of wood by cutting slots in them to match each other and inserting another piece, the tenon, as a joining piece between them.

OAR BLADE   flattened end of the oar that is pulled through the water for propulsion.

OAR GEARING   the ratio of the loom to the sweep of an oar.

OAR LOOM   the length of the oar shaft between the thole and the inboard end.

OAR-STROKE   one complete cycle of working an oar.

OAR SWEEP   the length of the oar shaft between the thole and the outboard end.

OAR-BOX   construction along the side of an ancient rowing ship to carry tholes out and beyond the ship's side.

OAR-PORT   hole cut in a hull side through which an oar can be worked.

OCULUS   the symbol of an eye, attached or painted on a ship's bow as a good luck token, to 'see' it through a safe voyage.

OUTBOARD   from the centre-line of a ship towards the outside of the hull.

OUTRIGGER   a construction extending outboard of the hull proper to carry, for example, a thole.

PENNANT STAFF   light spar from which pennants are flown.

PLANK-ON-FRAME   method of hull construction where a skeleton of frames is first erected and then covered by planking.

PONTOONS   floating platforms.

POOP/POOP DECK   after Latin, *puppis*; the aftermost top deck of a ship.

PORT   the left-hand side of a ship when viewed from the stern.

PROW   the bow section of a ship.

PUMP, CHAIN OR BUCKET   a string of containers attached to a moving belt around a top and bottom pivot, which are filled at the bottom of their travel and empty at the top when they tilt.

PUMP, DOUBLE-ACTING   a pump which operates through a system of valves so that it works on both the up and down strokes of the operating handle.

QUARTER   the rearmost side part of a ship.

QUAY   a solid platform projecting into the water for ships to come alongside.

RAIL   the top of a bulwark or framework on deck.

RAM   armoured, reinforced projection on the bow of a ship used to damage or puncture an enemy hull.

RATLINES   ropes tied horizontally across shrouds (q.v.) to act like the steps of a ladder.

REME   a horizontal level of rowers.

RIG   all of the ropes, sails and tackle needed to operate a ship when under sail.

RIGELS   'eyebrow'-type ridges above a port or hull opening to stop water from running down the hull side and inside.

RUDDER-BALANCED   where part of the rudder blade is in front of the shaft balancing the force of the water acting on the rear part to an extent.

RUDDER-STERN-HUNG   where a rudder is hung on pintles from the sternpost (q.v.).

RUDDERS/SIDE RUDDERS/STEERING OARS   steering devices affixed to the stern quarters (q.v.) of a ship on one or both sides.

RUNNING RIGGING   rigging which is used to operate the sails.

SAGGING   when the length of a ship hull is lifted at bow and stern by large waves, causing the mid section to drop, straining the hull; the opposite of hogging.

SETTLING (-IN THE WATER)   process whereby a ship sinks to the level of its latent buoyancy, dictated by the materials from which it is made.

SHEATHING   covering of the underwater part of a hull to deter marine parasites.

SHEETS   ropes attached to and used to control the bottom corners of a sail.

SHORTEN SAIL (TO)   to reduce the deployed area of a sail.

SHROUDS   supporting ropes or lines secured between a mast and the sides of a ship.

SKEG   metal or hardwood strips attached to the hull bottom to protect it when it is hauled ashore.

SPONSON   a platform projecting beyond the hull proper. See also jettied.

SQUARE RIG   where a yard and sail are rigged across the beam of a ship.

STANCHIONS   vertical struts or supports.

STANDING RIGGING   rigging used to support the mast(s).

STARBOARD   the right-hand side of a ship when viewed from the stern; after 'steering board', the side upon which a single side rudder was fixed.

STAYS   supporting ropes or lines between a mast and the bow (forestay) and stern (backstay) of a ship.

STEM   the bow of a ship (q.v.).

STEMPOST   the foremost vertical timber of the ship, forming the point of the bow.

STEPPED (MAST)   the act of erecting a mast. Mast step: mounting upon which the mast stands.

STERN   the rearmost part of a ship.

STERN QUARTERS   the rear flanks of a hull.

STERNPOST   the aftermost vertical timber of the ship.

STERNSHEETS   the aftermost inside part of an open boat.

STOCK (ANCHOR)   the horizontal bar across the top of an anchor.

STRAKE   a line of planking along the length of a hull.

STRIKING RATE   the frequency with which oar strokes are made.

SUPPARUM   triangular sails fitted above the yard and to the mast.

TABERNACLE   fitting or mounting securing the foot of a mast.

TACKLE   ropes for use with blocks.

TENDER, SHIP'S   a small boat used for errands by its parent ship.

THALAMITE   rower of the lowest reme in a trireme arrangement.

THOLE   the pin against which an oar is pivoted and worked.

THRANITE   rower of the topmost reme of a multi-reme ship.

THWARTS   timbers fitted between the sides of a hull as spacers stretching from side to side and doubling, for example, as seats.

TILLER   a bar inserted into a rudder shaft used to operate it.

TIPSTAFF   a type of tiller.

TOW   fibres of hemp or flax used for packing or caulking.

TREENAIL   wooden peg used as or as part of a fastening.

TRUSS   a wood or rope tie used to draw or hold parts together.

VENTILATION COURSE   a line of openings along the side of a hull to permit a flow of air to a rowing crew.

VEXILLUM   small flag or banner of a military detachment, including a warship.

WALE   strengthening or protective timber fitted along a length of the outside of a hull.

WATERLINE   the level to which a hull floats in the water.

WINDLASS/ WINCH   drum-like devices which are turned to wind or unwind ropes or cables.

YARD   pole or spar to which a sail is attached.

ZYGITE   rower in the middle reme in a trireme arrangement.

BIBLIOGRAPHY

PRIMARY SOURCES

Appian *The Civil Wars*. Trans. John Carter.
Caesar *The Battle for Gaul*. Trans. A. and P. Wiseman.
Caesar *The Civil War*. Trans. F. P. Long.
Dio Cassius *Roman History*. Trans. Ian Scott-Kilvert and John Carter.
Herodotus *The Histories*. Trans. G. Rawlinson.
Homer *The Iliad*. Trans. E. V. Rieu.
Homer *The Odyssey*. Trans. E. V. Rieu and D. C. H. Rieu.
Livy *The History of Rome (Ad Urbe Condita Libri)*. Books I–V: *The Early History of Rome*. Books XXI–XXX: *The War with Hannibal*. Trans. A. De Selincourt.
Pliny *Natural History*. Trans. John Healey.
Polybius *The Rise of the Roman Empire*. Trans. I. Scott-Kilvert.
Procopius *The Vandalic Wars*. Trans. H. B. Dewing.
Silius Italicus *Punica*. Trans. J. D. Duff.
Tacitus *The Agricola*. Trans. H. Mattingley.
Tacitus *The Annals*. Trans. M. Grant.
Tacitus *The Histories*. Trans. K. Wellesley.
Thucydides *The Peloponnesian War*. Trans. B. Jowett.
Vegetius *Epitome of Military Science*. Trans. N. P. Milner.
Xenophon *The Persian Expedition*. Trans. R. Warner.
Zosimus *New History*. Trans. Ronald T. Ridley.

OTHER SOURCES

Anderson R. C. *Oared Fighting Ships*. Argus Books 1976.
Austin N. J. E. and Rankov N. B. *Exploratio: Military and Political Intelligence in the Roman World from the Second Punic War to the Battle of Adrianople*. Routledge 1995.
Bascom W. *Deep Water, Ancient Ships*. David & Charles 1976.
Bass G. F., ed. *A History of Seafaring Based on Underwater Archaeology*. Thames and Hudson 1972.
Bounegru O. and Zahariade M. *Les Forces Navales du Bas Danube et de la Mer Noire aux Ier–VIe Siècles*. Oxbow Books 1996.
Casson L. *Ships and Seamanship in the Ancient World*. Princeton University Press 1986.
Casson L. *Ships and Seafaring in Ancient Times*. British Museum Press 1994.
Casson L. and Steffy J. R. *The Athlit Ram*. Texas A & M University Press 1991.
Conway's *The Age of the Galley*. Conway Maritime Press 1995.
Ellmers D. 'Celtic Planked Ships 500 BC to AD 1000', in *The Earliest Ships: The Evolution of Boats into Ships*, ed. R. Gardiner and A.E. Christensen. Conway Maritime Press 2004.
Frost H. 'The Punic Wreck in Sicily', *International Journal of Naval Archaeology*, 3(1), 35–54, 1974.
Grainge G. *The Roman Invasion of Britain*. Tempus 2005.

Guilmartin J. F. *Galleons and Galleys*. Cassell & Co. 2002.

Guilmartin J. F. *Gunpowder and Galleys*. Conway Maritime Press 2003.

Haywood J. *Dark Age Naval Power*. Anglo-Saxon Books 1999.

Johnston P. F. *Ship and Boat Models in Ancient Greece*. Naval Institute Press 1985.

Marsden E. W. *Greek and Roman Artillery, Historical Development*. Oxford University Press 1969.

Marsden E. W. *Greek and Roman Artillery, Technical Treatises*. Oxford University Press 1971.

Marsden P. 'Ships of the Roman Period and After', in Bass, *A History of Seafaring*.

Meijer F. *A History of Seafaring in the Classical World*. Croom Helm 1986.

Morrison J and Coates J. *Greek and Roman Oared Warships*. Oxbow Books 1996.

Morrison J., Coates J. and Rankov N. B. *The Athenian Trireme*. Cambridge University Press 2000.

Ormerod D. *Piracy in the Ancient World*. Johns Hopkins University Press 1997.

Pitassi M. P. *The Navies of Rome*. Boydell & Brewer 2009.

Rodgers W. L. *Greek and Roman Naval Warfare*. Naval Institute Press 1964.

Russo F. and Russo F. *89 A.C. Assiedo a Pompeii*. Edizioni Flavius 2005.

Scullard H. H. *A History of the Roman World, 753 to 146 BC*, 4th edition. Routledge 1991.

Severin T. *The Jason Voyage*. Hutchinson & Co. 1985.

Sprague de Camp L. *The Ancient Engineers*. Ballantine 1963.

Starr C. G. *The Roman Imperial Navy*. Ares Publishers 1993.

Tilley A. *Seafaring on the Ancient Mediterranean*. British Archaeological Reports 2004.

Thubron C. *The Seafarers: Ancient Mariners*. Time-Life Books 1981.

Torr C. *Ancient Ships*. Argonaut 1964.

Ward C. A. *Sacred and Secular: Ancient Egyptian Ships and Boats*. Archaeological Institute of America 2000.

Welsh F. *Building the Trireme*. Constable & Co. 1988.

INDEX